Shanghai Doctor

An American Physician Confronts Communist China

Nicholas Comninellis

ZondervanPublishingHouse
Grand Rapids, Michigan

A Division of HarperCollinsPublishers

Published by Zondervan Publishing House
1415 Lake Drive, S.E., Grand Rapids, Michigan 49506

Library of Congress Cataloging-in-Publication Data

Comninellis, Nicholas.
   Shanghai doctor / by Nicholas Comninellis.
     p. cm.
   ISBN 0-310-53211-6
    1. Comninellis, Nicholas. 2. Missionaries, Medical—United
States—Biography. 3. Missionaries, Medical—China—Shanghai—
Biography. I. Title.
R722.32.C64A3   1991
610.69'5'092—dc20
+[B]   90–45156
                                                  CIP

Edited by Lori Walburg

Printed in the United States of America

91 92 93 94 95 / EE / 5 4 3 2 1

SHANGHAI DOCTOR

Contents

Preface

One of the characteristics of my life is that it has been unpredictable. If someone had told me when I graduated from high school that I'd become the first American physician to have a full-time position in China since their Communist revolution, I would have said they were dreaming. But sometimes dreams come true.

If someone had said that I'd live with my wife and two preschool children in war-torn Angola as one of the two hundred physicians in that vast African nation, I'd have said they were crazy. But sometimes what seems crazy is most expedient.

I'm here in Angola today, working with the Christians in the city of Huambo to organize simple clinics to care for the multitude of citizens with little or no health-care. Our clinics are held in church buildings not only because our resources are limited, but also for a very symbolic reason: Health care and Christian ministry are very compatible. In both areas we see broken people healed.

The person who is physically sick or injured can be treated and nursed to wholeness. Likewise, the one who is separated from Jesus Christ can hear of his love, decide to believe, and be healed spiritually. It has been a wonderful, if sometimes painful, experience to participate in this type of comprehensive ministry.

I can not predict accurately where I'll live or in what situation I'll work in the future, but one thing is certain: No matter where we are, the love of Jesus Christ for each one of us is unfailing, penetrating, exuberant, and life changing!

Acknowledgments

The events described in this book occurred in 1982 and 1983 in Shanghai, China. The names of the characters and details of some of the events have been altered to protect the identity of the persons involved.

I am deeply grateful to the Shanghai Ren Ji Hospital, the Shanghai Second Medical College, and the University of Missouri at Kansas City School of Medicine. Without their constant cooperation none of the events described herein would have been possible.

SHANGHAI
DOCTOR

Prologue

*L*USH AND GREEN, the fields of tender rice spread across the horizon, broken up only by waterways branching to the mighty Chang Jiang River. It was early morning. Dew clung to the rice shoots and sparkled with the sunrise.

Here amid the young stems, ankle deep in muddy water, stood a small team of peasants digging in the soft mud. They were planting rice shoots. One after another, each worker reached into the rugged sack on his back and chose a shoot from among the hundreds he carried. Clad in long, fading shirts, the peasants inched along their rows with their eyes fixed to the earth. The sun rose higher, and soon the wet field was enveloped in a fog of steam.

The sun seemed an added burden to Li Ming. His heart began to pound unnaturally. Unusual, he thought, that fatigue should overtake him so early in the day. His trim body ordinarily carried him through the most intense labor of harvest. He still considered himself to be young—only forty-five years old, not even at his prime yet. But his heart continued its loud pounding, so he eased the heavy sack from his shoulder and slowly sat down on the earth. The mud oozed between his toes. After a few moments, the other peasants had moved on down their rows and were lost from sight in the fog.

Li Ming did not want to be left too far behind. He took his sack in one hand and started to rise. His spinning head told him this was not a good idea, yet he persisted. His other hand clutched his wobbling knees and slowly his back straightened toward the sky. Then his sight went black. His limp body fell to the ground with a soft splash.

The sun continued to climb the oriental sky, beating down more strongly on the group of workers who continued planting. They paused now and then to wipe the sweat from their brows and look back on the long rows of newly planted rice. When they came to the shade of a lonely tree, they stopped and rested a moment, passing a small cloth canteen among them.

"What has become of Li Ming?" asked one of them suddenly as he waited his turn with the canteen. "I have not seen him for some time."

"Didn't he return to bring out more shoots?" replied another, taking a long swig from the canteen before passing it on.

One of the men leaned against the tree. Shading his eyes, he looked out over the fields. "No, no. Look. Far behind us. Isn't that him out there?"

The other laborers stood there and peered over at the figure. "Well, that isn't fair. He is sleeping, and we are doing all the work!"

"He is like a brother to me," said a young man. "I will go see what he is up to." He trotted off toward the distant figure sprawled in the mud.

The others watched. "Li is a good man. It is not like him to try to get out of work," said one.

"You are right," added another. "I can remember when he came to help me cut grass for the roof of my house. There are few like him."

They continued to watch as the young man, now far off, crouched over Li. After a moment he quickly rose and let out a shout that brought the others hurrying to the spot. When they arrived, they found Li gasping for breath. His body burned with fever, and his arms and legs hung useless at his sides. Though they pleaded with him to speak, he couldn't. His glassy eyes seemed to stare right through them.

"What can we do?" cried one. "He could die any moment now. What will I tell his wife?"

"We must get him to a doctor," said the young man.

"But where is there any doctor? There is no hospital for miles."

"I know, I know, but there is one chance." He stood and pointed to the north. "We can take him to the city."

The others nodded in agreement, and the strongest among them lifted Li onto his back. They headed toward a water canal and halted a passing barge carrying fruit down the river.

The man carrying Li called out, "Stop your boat! You must help us!"

The captain turned his back on them. "No. I must get these crops to the market before they spoil."

"This is more important than your profit," Li's friend shouted. "This man is very ill. Do not disgrace your name by acting so!"

The other peasants joined in, "You will be a shame to the country! We know who you are!"

At this, the captain guided his craft to the bank and took on the dying man. The peasants laid Li Ming under a canopy on the deck and moistened his face with some water from the canal. A straw mat separated him from the rough wood deck. One of the peasants sat and fanned him as they shoved off from shore.

At the rear of the boat stood one man, weaving the oar

from side to side. For the rest of the day they crawled along at a snail's pace. Finally, as sunset approached, the captain caught sight of the harbor in the distance and let out a shout.

They had reached Shanghai.

One Revolution
Around the Globe

*E*VERY MORNING WE BEGAN with rounds. The
young Chinese doctors and I made our way from bed
to bed in the long, crowded wards of Shanghai's most
prominent general hospital. Set in the old part of the city, the
Third People's Hospital stood far above the sea of brick
houses that surrounded it. Although it was still early, the
doors and windows were spread open to catch any breeze that
might blow, for the heat was smoldering. Dr. Tao, our
medical department chief, stood in the midst of our group. As
we passed by the beds of our patients we discussed their care,
one by one.

We paused at the side of one elderly man suffering from
rheumatic fever. He lay on a rusty iron bed with a cushion
under his head. He looked up with surprise as I approached
to examine him.

"You are a foreigner!" he said in Chinese. "I have never had
a foreign doctor before. This is quite unusual." I nodded and
smiled, accustomed by now to Chinese reactions to my
presence. "Why have you come to China?" he asked.

I could see the other doctors looking our way as they
waited for my reply. I answered, "I am an American, a guest
in your country. You Chinese have a very different social
system and view of life from ours in America. I am curious to
know about your people and customs. I have come to be your

friend and learn from your people." I felt a little awkward with this reply, for it did not reveal all of my real intentions.

The man was taken aback. He shook his head and said, "In America, I am told, you have cars and magnificent entertainment and every kind of freedom. Most of these men here would give almost anything to go to America, yet you have come to us. This is strange indeed."

The group of doctors continued to listen with interest. The old man raised his hand. "Dr. Kong, if you will learn from us, then I will be one of your teachers. We are the most mighty and wise people in the world. We have the answers to the greatest questions there are. Listen to the story that my people will tell you. Our history is the longest of any on earth, and our culture goes deep to the origins of mankind itself." He sat up on one elbow and pointed a finger. "My family has been in Shanghai for more than six hundred years, through wars and epidemics, through famine and revolution, yet we survive. We are a proud people, proved by our art and families, yet humbled through repeated tragedy. You are fortunate to be here!"

Just then a nurse dressed in white hastily approached us. "There is a critical case just arrived that you must see at once."

Dr. Tao and I hurried down a dark staircase in the ancient building and found our way to the bustling emergency room. There were hundreds standing in line in an open courtyard, waiting for treatment. In spite of the apparent disorder, we were directed to a corner, where we saw a pathetic figure lying on the bare floor. Several peasants stood around him. One said that the man's name was Li Ming.

He did not stir as we approached. His patched, bleached overalls were soaked with sweat, and his wet skin glistened in the dim light. Someone momentarily arrived with a stretcher, and Li Ming was carried to another room for treatment.

As we started an IV to provide drugs for his failing heart, I said to Dr. Tao, "This is strange. He seems to be suffering from a heart attack, but then why is his temperature 105 degrees? I have never seen an illness like this in America." My own heart was pounding from the excitement of facing my first real emergency case since my arrival in China a few weeks earlier.

Bent over his patient, probing with a stethoscope, Dr. Tao listened closely to Li's pounding heart. Then he straightened, removing the instrument from his ears before answering. "It is because his heart is infected with a virus. The virus damages and weakens the heart and makes it beat poorly. I understand that this condition is rare in your country, but here you will see this often. We will treat him with dan sun."

Puzzled, I shook my head. Then I said a familiar phrase, already used many times in my short time in China: "What is that? I never heard of it in my medical school."

"It is an herb that increases the strength of the heart," Dr. Tao explained. "We have many more traditional drugs like this. They can be better than any other medications you know about. Come now, we will give him a gram and see his response." The nurse standing by left for the pharmacy to get the drug, and Dr. Tao and I watched over the man.

"Where did you learn about these drugs?" I asked.

"It is part of the curriculum in our medical schools, along with anatomy, chemistry, and the rest," Tao said. "We also believe in a well-rounded education. As part of our training we also study politics in depth several hours a week. In class I have read the works of Marx and Mao Tse-tung. They are the principles we go by, but still, it's rather hard to apply the principles of dialectical materialism in the hospital."

"How interesting!" I replied. "My education was pretty sterile in comparison. So you actually dealt with questions of philosophy and politics in medical school. That seems very wise."

A shy nurse hovered behind us, waiting for our attention before she spoke. "A woman is here, who just came from the countryside. She says that she is the wife of your patient, Li Ming."

Behind her followed a very attractive woman dressed in green coveralls, with black hair braided into a ponytail that hung down her back. Canvas shoes covered her feet. When she saw Li, she cried out and hurried to his side. She clutched him and began to weep loudly.

Dr. Tao motioned to me to come close, and he said in a low voice, "Dr. Kong, here in China our spouses mean everything to us. We have a proverb that says that marriage is like having heaven on earth. She will cry, yet she will control her grief in a short time."

After a moment Li's wife looked up. She quickly brushed the tears from her eyes and regained her composure somewhat. Turning to me, she said in a clear voice, "I don't understand this. My husband's health has always been good. He has worked in the fields for years, and now he does not even recognize who I am." She paused and her lip began to quiver. "What can I tell our daughter?"

I touched her shoulder. It was hard to know what to say. "Li is a strong man. We will do all that we can to help him through this." I explained his condition to her, but I felt that my description did not help her much. I had always had trouble delivering bad news.

Her eyes were still showing her agony as she returned to Li Ming's side. On the wall behind them was painted a political slogan: "Hold high the banner of Marxism." I stood back from them, looking around at the people in the emergency room. There was a wizened old man puffing on a local cigarette. Plump babies were nursing from their mothers. Eastern music played from a transistor radio. For a moment it all seemed as strange as it had on that first day when I arrived in Shanghai to serve as a medical intern. . . .

I awoke from an uncomfortable sleep and looked out of the window. The sky was as clear and blue as the sea below it. Looking up, I saw the moon still in plain view, and even some of the stars from the quickly fading night hanging on into the light of morning. Below, the sea was speckled with white caps that loomed larger as our jet descended toward the jagged coastline. Amid the mountains below perched a white city, spreading to engulf the tiny peninsula on which she sat. As I looked down, my pulse began to race. After years of preparation I was almost there! Hong Kong: the last outpost before China itself!

I was still breathless from the whirl of festivities and packing that surrounded graduation from medical school. Only two weeks earlier I had stood in robes with my class and taken the oath of physicians. We had sworn to be compassionate, to live by the highest morals, to be no respecter of persons, and to honor our teachers. I had also made a promise to Jesus Christ to share my faith as I worked, wherever I might be. How successful I was to be at fulfilling these oaths remained to be seen.

Just before I left, I had lunch with my sister Daphne for the last time. She was just about to start fifth grade, and I thought the world of her. She made fun of me for shaving off my full beard. As I explained to her that it wouldn't be appropriate for me to wear a beard in China, I realized how much I would miss her. I also knew that I'd miss my friends at Cornerstone, my home church. They had prayed for me before I left and promised to keep it up.

I faced many difficult questions when I decided to go to China. Several asked, "Have you decided to become a Communist?" Others were more pragmatic: "What can you possibly learn from the Chinese? Their technology is nothing like ours." My mother hit a delicate spot when she asked, "Won't you be lonely?" But the most vicious accusation was "Look, you're wasting a year of your life!" I heard it from many professors and friends, and it made me want to avoid seeing them or even saying good-bye. Even my Chinese language tutor was not sure of the wisdom of my going.

Everyone else from school was off to do residency training in a particular medical specialty. I had decided to take an unprecedented step and defer this phase of my training for a year. The founder of my school, E. Gray Dimond, had strong friendships in the medical community inside China and had helped me to visit Shanghai for a medical elective as part of my education a year earlier. When I was invited by the Chinese to return, he arranged for me to go back and spend a year there as an exchange between our medical centers. It had not been done before, but this did not bother me.

I had other reasons for going in addition to my curiosity about China. After years of living surrounded by books and the secluded little world of medicine, I felt that I needed to take a break and see some of the real world. I often thought, *Sure, I know a lot of facts about health care, but there are other things that I know nothing about. I want to take time to experience some of the adventure of life!*

Throughout my time in medical school I also had a growing concern: the social inequalities and injustice I had seen in America. I lived near the medical center, which was situated on a hill. On one side of the hill was the most fabulous shopping, hotel, and entertainment complex in the city. It was a place of big money and fancy cars. I enjoyed walking through it though I possessed neither big money nor a fancy car.

But on the other side of the hill, equally visible from my window, was a city ghetto area. Unemployed men prowled the dusty streets day and night. Their children were often malnourished, and invariably filthy. It seemed as though someone was stabbed or shot every night in the neighborhood. I knew about their situation because they came to the hospital where I was a student. I knew that they were no better off than millions of others, but they were extremely visible to me. I felt sorry for them. Their cycle of poverty seemed endless, each new generation taking on the habits of those before them. Sometimes I wondered whether those who were better off would, or could, help them out.

Next to the shopping complex stood a plush hospital that served the more well-to-do of the city. We went there for part of our training as well. One night a twelve-year-old black girl was walking in front of this hospital with some of her friends. A car drove past and a man with a gun fired three shots into the group. The girl crumpled to the sidewalk. The others screamed and ran inside to tell the receptionist. There was an ambulance parked in front of the emergency room at the back of the hospital. In two or three minutes it arrived on the scene.

The girl was crying. Her blood pressure was low, and three large holes in her abdomen were bleeding. The medics quickly loaded her into their truck and drove back to the emergency room door, one half block away. The doors burst open as they wheeled her in for help, but they were stopped short. Before them, dressed in a dark suit, stood a cool administrator.

"Wait a moment!" he said. "What's going on here?"

The medics came to a reluctant halt. "This girl is shot bad! She needs attention now. Now let's get going." The medic started to push by the man.

"Not so fast. Look at her." His eyes ran down the girl's body. Her clothes were dirty and tattered, her hair was uncut, and there was an unpleasant odor. "We can't accept any more charity patients this month. We already filled our quota."

"Look, she's hurt bad," the medic insisted. "She's bleeding internally and needs to be seen at once!"

"Now you look," the administrator said, getting defensive, "she's awake. She'll be okay. Take her to the city hospital. You can be there in ten minutes. Now get out!"

The medics reluctantly turned around and rolled her back to their truck. They were angry, bitterly angry at the refusal, for it was obvious to them that she was getting worse.

I met them when they arrived in our emergency room fifteen minutes later. They rushed inside and there was a whirl of action around her as the physicians and nurses tried to resuscitate her. As I stood by her, she looked up at me.

"Please don't let me die!" she whispered. That was the last thing she said. She died five minutes later.

At first, I wept. Then word came to us of where she had been taken first and I was mad—fighting mad. I turned on my surgery resident, demanding answers. "Here we are, trying to take care of people, and someone is out there taking potshots at little girls. Then, just because she's poor and black, the people who could have saved her kick her out. What can we do to stop things like this from happening?"

He shook his head and laughed cynically. "There's nothing you can do. It's human nature—some of it is good, some bad. Just get used to it and don't let it bother you. Remember, we're just here to pick up the pieces."

I could not swallow his prescription. Later, in my room, I

pondered the incident. *People today are still struggling with the same problems of human nature that they always have*, I thought. *Technology has not made it any better. Look at all of the wars, the poverty, and the unhappy people. I'm not just going to accept it as it is.* In church we talked about loving others as much as Jesus did, but it didn't seem as though enough people were taking this idea seriously. I hoped that in China I'd have time to think about these issues. While I was skeptical of the answers Marxism offered to solve social problems, I still thought that I could learn something from the Chinese.

Even so, I realized that I was taking a risky step into the unknown. One night shortly before I left, my roommate encouraged me: "Nick, what you're doing others don't understand. There is a vast world out there that few of us have any idea of. Here in America, we live isolated lives and are consumed pretty much with our own happiness, but beyond our borders, there are people who live with ideas and beauty that we cannot comprehend. So—go for it. What you'll gain in China can't be measured in dollars or diplomas. It's worth far more."

Our plane swooped down and touched on the runway that jutted out into the harbor like a dock for ships of the sky. We bounced once, then coasted toward the airport gates.

"Dr. Comninellis!" a voice called out as I emerged from the doorway. I looked out into the crowd to see who it was. A man kept calling my name, so I walked toward him. Before me stood the Chinese gentleman with whom I had corresponded for months beforehand. He wore a pressed white shirt that hung out around the waist of his short pants. His smile told me that I had won my first friend in the East.

"Welcome to Hong Kong! It's fine to see you at last."

We shook hands. "Pao Chu, you look as lively as I imagined. I appreciate your coming to meet me. I had a good long trip to think about what I was getting into!"

"Well, I have appreciated the letters that you sent to me," he said. "Where will you be staying?"

"I have a reservation at the YMCA."

"Good! That is close by."

We picked up my two bags and caught a cab, which took us winding through the narrow streets. People dressed in brightly colored clothes swarmed over the sidewalks. Chinese-character neon signs blinked above us, and English-style double-decker buses filled the roads. Skyscrapers towered on either side and darkened the streets. Laundry hung from poles above our heads and swayed in the sea breeze.

The cab stopped at the downtown YMCA where I had reserved a simple room for three dollars a night. In the lobby were travelers from all over the world, and I counted at least six languages being spoken. Across the street some blond, tanned European backpackers sat in an ornate oriental restaurant. The concept of the community of the world seemed to be a reality here. *Boy*, I thought, *this is going to be a more interesting year than my friends will have back home!*

Pao Chu then offered to take me on a short tour of the city. We bought tickets on the Star Ferry to visit the lighthouse at the island's peak. We headed toward Hong Kong Island, the boat rocking gently in the clear water. A small flock of sea gulls followed along behind, scavenging for food.

I turned to my companion. "I am so happy that my language tutor gave me your name before I left. It is a real treat to know someone here."

"Oh, Dr. Comninellis, it is my pleasure. I am happy to be a part of your little expedition into China. You see, I am interested to hear about what you will find there."

"I'll let you know. You said that you are from China originally. How was it that you came to Hong Kong?"

"That was quite a long time ago," he replied. "I was a peasant in the Su Zhou province of China for many years. There were several hundred of us who worked for a landlord in his grape orchard. My wife and three children lived in a sod house, and all five of us worked from before sunrise until late at night just to survive."

"That sounds terrible," I said.

Pao Chu nodded. "Fifty percent of the harvest we had to give to the landlord, and besides that, we had to pay rent for the house. When winter came, there was no heat. One of my daughters died from the cold."

"Wasn't there anything that you could do for help? What about friends? Couldn't they give you fuel? How about the landlord?"

"Nothing. The landlord had complete control of my life as well as the lives of my friends. We belonged to him. He did not care. We were allowed only a certain amount of wood to burn. When that was gone there was no more. There were many landlords, and each one's land was like a small kingdom in itself. Once, another landlord attacked us. My son, who was only thirteen, was forced to serve in the army. He was armed with only a simple spear and went out too young to understand the cruelty of men. He never came back." Pao Chu fell into a sad silence.

The boat began to sway more as the tide came in. We clutched the side rail and hung on. Pao was looking down at the water with a furrowed brow. When he spoke again, his voice was low and tense.

"One thing that you need to understand is how Buddhism affected me and other Chinese. Part of the teaching was that we were simply to serve our masters, the landlords, and not question authority. We existed only for this purpose. The leadership of our masters was said to be somehow eternally ordained. We dared not resist it. I would go to the temple almost daily and pray to the Buddha for some freedom, but there was never a reply.

"But one day something happened. A man came to our village and talked about all of us peasants getting together and fighting against the landlords. He said that there were many others who were behind him. They had overthrown the power of their landlords already. The man's name was Sun Yat-sen. We now call him the George Washington of China. He was young then, and we followed him with all our hearts. He made promises to us. He promised that the land would belong to all of us. We would all share the tools and divide up the harvest among us. This way our families would have enough food. He said that we would be our own rulers and have a democratic state where everyone had a voice."

"It sounds like for the first time you had real hope," I said. "You must have been inspired."

"I certainly was! I left my family for a time and joined his army. We fought against the landlords and the old Chinese empire. We also fought against the foreigners who had established colonies in China: the French, English, and Portuguese. We were indeed liberating China from all those who had controlled us."

A heavy wooden houseboat drifted by, raising its bamboo sail to the wind. It picked up speed and passed our ferry. A string of old barges began to pass by the ferry as well. We stopped talking, distracted for a moment by the sights. I turned toward Pao Chu. "It must have been an exciting time to live. But why did you decide to leave your home for Hong Kong?"

"It is an involved story. After the war for independence I

returned to my town. They honored me like a true hero! We rebuilt our community, and for the first time everyone had enough to eat. There was peace for a number of years. But then things began to change. It has always been a part of human nature that people like power. Greed and self-interest are still prime movers. The Japanese began to invade China in the 1930s. They wanted to expand their own empire. They took the oil-rich land of northeastern China and then came down the coast and occupied cities. We were terrified of them—they were so strong!

"One day, they came near our town. We tried to run away from them, for we had no weapons. But they surrounded us, beat us, and marched us to the center of town. We thought that we would be safe there. Once we got there, though, the Japanese simply lined us up and shot us with machine guns. There was blood and screaming everywhere! Somehow, they missed me, but I fell down like the others and pretended to be dead. After dark, I managed to get back to my home. My wife said that many of the women had been raped and then buried alive."

Now Pao was clutching the side rail of the boat, tense, as if reliving the event. Sweat was running down his face, though the day was cool. "We decided that moment that we had to leave. For three weeks we traveled by foot, mostly at night so as not to be seen. Once when some soldiers stopped us, I had my daughter wrapped up as if she were sick, and they let us go on. We ate rice balls that were baked before we left. When they were gone, we just went hungry.

"At last we came to a great river, which separated the Japanese occupied territory from the rest of China. The river bank was guarded by a fence and dogs. A sign said that anyone trying to escape would be shot on sight, but we certainly could not go back. The only alternative was to try to swim across. The water was frigid, and we were very tired from the walking. My remaining daughter was only two and a half then. Still, we had no choice but to try. Late one night, the three of us slid into the water and began to swim to freedom. We were about two hundred feet from shore when a guard shined a light on us and began to shoot. The bullets splashed all around us. I held my child on my chest to protect her. My wife screamed, and then I felt terrible pain in my back. Blood was running from a rip in my shirt. My mind began to fade after a moment, and I felt the water come over my head and my daughter choking in my arms."

Pao stopped and wiped the sweat from his face. In the background we could hear a tug with a lone diesel engine, chugging at the rate of a rapid heartbeat. "My wife is a small woman, but she took my chin by one hand and the girl in the other and propelled the three of us with her legs until the spotlight was far away. The bullets still pelted the water but were far off their target. We crawled up onto the other side of the river bank. Then I collapsed and remember nothing more for several days. But we were free!"

Just then our ferry reached the island, and the sailors on board cast their ropes to the dock to secure the boat. After disembarking, we climbed aboard a trolley car that took us up the steep mountainside for a look at Hong Kong Island.

Pao looked intently across the mountains as we rode. The buildings along the coast grew smaller and smaller as we rose toward the clouds. A stately lighthouse crowned the top of the peak. Here Pao and I got off the trolley to watch the sun set between the mountains.

"Pao Chu," I said in a moment of inspiration, "do you suppose that there is a solution for people acting so badly toward one another?" Unlike the surgery resident, he did not laugh at my question.

"I am not sure. I've asked myself that question before. We would need to change human nature to start with." He paused. "Over there, in the distance, is China." He waved his right hand toward the north. "I have heard that the leaders there are making some efforts to do just that. I wonder how successful they have been? I may one day find out, for soon Hong Kong will be part of China again."

"What do you mean?"

"The British leased Hong Kong Island and the nearby peninsula from the Chinese. That lease expires in 1997. All of this wealth will then belong to China."

Pao continued to look intently across the mountains. The salty breeze blew his hair into tangles. The two of us turned and walked back to the trolley. I stopped as we boarded to take one last look over the mountains.

Pao noticed my gaze. When I turned toward him again, he looked at me solemnly, then said, "If you find the answer to your question in China, you must tell me."

"I will," I promised.

Dr. Kong

*T*HE SMALL VAN LURCHED along a tree-lined back road that wound from the small military airport to one of the world's largest, most congested cities. We passed cultivated fields and small factories. The crowds grew thicker as the city approached. They began to flow into the streets, and we had to swerve to avoid them. Most were dressed in dull blue or green army clothes, but occasionally I saw a young woman wearing a colored silk coat. We passed several tractors on the road towing wagons of fruit, and peasants lay amid the apples and oranges in back. China was a far cry from Hong Kong. I seemed to have stepped back fifty years in time.

Our van slowed momentarily as a little parade of young people carrying colorful cloths, pillows, and an electric fan crossed our path.

"Who are these people?" I asked the driver of the van, who had been sent to pick me up.

He looked surprised. "They are probably friends of some newlyweds, helping to carry home their wedding gifts. Where did you learn to speak Chinese? Very few of our foreign visitors do."

"I studied in America. Listen, why don't these people use a car to haul the things home?"

"All of the cars are controlled by the government. We can't

own one. Besides, none of us could afford to use one. But I feel fortunate to have this job driving a car."

Just then a modern bus, full of richly dressed tourists, rushed by. The driver watched them go. He commented, "These foreigners are usually allowed to see only the best things in China. In fact, only a few cities in China are open for foreigners to visit. But you—it will be different with you. You will be living among us."

The roadside was lined as far as the eye could-see with small wooden houses. They were built against one another, each with a single door leading in. Their red tile roofs sloped over the pavement below, where women sat washing clothes in large pans or spread grain on towels to dry. In a park elderly men dressed in identical blue jackets huddled in packs, playing cards. Others in the park carried pet birds in cages to air them, as one might walk a dog. On a corner, schoolgirls were clapping a rhythm and jumping rope. Their book bags were piled on the street beside them. Around their necks hung identical red scarfs.

"What are the scarves for?" I asked.

"All of the schoolchildren in China must wear them. It is to remind them of the blood of the martyrs of the Communist revolution." The driver stared straight ahead. He did not seem to be impressed with the idea.

Passing over a bridge on the Suzhou River, our rickety van shoved its way through the most congested portion of Shanghai. Here markets filled the streets, which were blocked by lines of women waiting to buy food. I saw cabbages, onions, mushrooms, tomatoes, lettuce, cauliflower, and dozens of other vegetables that have no English equivalents. Stacks of pig carcasses lay on the ground by a butcher shop, with a boy sitting on top, swatting the flies away. The aroma of cut flowers mingled with the stench of rotting meat.

We pulled to a stop to let an electric trolley bus ahead finish loading. At each of its three wide doors people shoved and fought to board, while others pushed to get off, everyone exchanging curses and threats. After a moment, the disgusted conductor closed the doors on the throng. The bus then proceeded to the next station, where the performance was repeated. Later during my work at the hospital, I would treat bus passengers for rib fractures sustained in these bus battles.

The driver turned into a small alley that is Shan Dong Road and pointed to my new headquarters just ahead—the Third People's Hospital. Its tall red brick walls loomed high above the surrounding homes and storefronts. We drove through a large iron gate opening into a courtyard, bordered on three sides by the H-shaped hospital building. Above us, balconies hung from each of the seven floors. The balconies extended around the entire building, and in their shade, dozens of patients in gray hospital clothes sat looking down on us.

The van pulled to a stop, and a distinguished elderly man walked up to the door. He seemed to have been waiting for me. He was dressed in a plain white shirt that hung out about his waist, and his gray short pants ended halfway down to his knees. I felt very conspicuous in my suit and tie. As I stepped out, he introduced himself as Dr. Cheng Hui Xing, the director of the hospital. He seemed to glow with excitement.

"Welcome to China, Dr. Comninellis." His English was flawless. "This is the first time in thirty-five years that a Western doctor has actually been allowed to work in my country, and of all places, you have come to work here!" He smiled from ear to ear. "Please come inside." The driver explained to me that he would take my suitcases to my dorm.

As we walked Dr. Cheng said, "My professors at the university in the 1920s were from America, and I've looked forward for years to working with an American again. You probably know that we have been isolated from the rest of the world for a long time, but now this is starting to change. I hope that you will be the first of many Americans to live in China."

We walked through an entrance with two stone pillars on either side, then headed down a crowded hallway. "Let me show you around," Dr. Cheng said. "Your name, Comninellis, that's Greek, isn't it?"

I nodded. "Yes. My father came to America as a young man. He was surprised that I wanted to leave America to come to China."

Dr. Cheng looked amused. "Well, there is a spirit of adventure in all of us." He looked at me appraisingly. "We need to give you a good Chinese name. After all, you will be with us for a year." He paused and thought for a moment. A jackhammer in the courtyard started to pound, and I held my ears. "Oh, don't mind the noise. We are always fixing something." He held up a hand. "I have it. I will call you Dr. Kong. Kong means health. You not only look healthy, but as a physician you can give health to others." He paused and added thoughtfully, "—sometimes."

We walked into the hospital and down a corridor congested with patients in gray gowns and their families. Construction workers were repairing the peeling plaster on the walls, and we occasionally dodged a large sterilizer or pile of bamboo scaffolding poles stacked in the passage. There didn't seem to be any other place to store them.

The first area we reached was the pediatric ward. The children playing on the floor immediately dropped their toys to examine the strange-looking foreigner, giggling when I spoke their language with a Midwestern drawl.

Each child had a separate bed frame covered with a thin mattress and spread with a straw mat worn soft by years of use. In the intense heat of summer, Dr. Cheng explained, the children preferred to lie on a mat rather than on cotton sheets that clung to their skin. On a stand next to each bed was a thermos bottle and cup. It was strange to see these things on such a hot day.

"Why the thermos bottle in the middle of summer?" I asked.

"We boil all of our drinking water first, to purify it," said Dr. Cheng. "Before we began doing this typhoid fever, cholera, and dysentery were very common, but not anymore."

A pretty girl motioned to sit on my lap, then handed me a comic book to read to the group of youngsters. The sentences were written from the top down and read right to left. My head started to throb after a moment as I turned the pages and read aloud the hundreds of different characters that made up the story. Each character was like a tiny picture of its own. When I finished, the children applauded wildly and said that I was the biggest comic they'd seen in months. They gave me a rousing "bye-bye" in English as I left, which quite surprised me. Later, I learned that Chinese children use this phrase commonly.

Dr. Cheng had been standing quietly by the doorway. We proceeded on down the hall. "This is an ancient city you are in," he said, "and these children are but one of a multitude of generations who have lived here."

"I think that they are better off now than before," I said, remembering my conversation with Pao Chu.

"Yes, they are. For thousands of years China was ruled by a series of empires or dynasties. We developed our own culture and history quite apart from the rest of the world. During the Tang Dynasty, 1800 years ago, people first settled along the banks of the Huangpu River, and that became Shanghai. Their homes have been here ever since."

"What does the word *Shanghai* mean?"

"Literally translated, it means 'above the ocean.' You see, the city is just above where the river empties into the Pacific, so we are indeed above the ocean."

We passed the accounting office where the *click click* of an abacus filled the air. *Technology has not come here yet,* I thought. *I bet that they have done it this way for centuries.*

"What was life like in those days?" I asked.

"For most people it was very difficult. They were terribly poor and lived on small plots of land growing whatever they could. Drought and the battling landlords were a constant threat. Food was often scarce. Wars were a continual problem. In fact, the Great Wall in northern China was built to prevent the relentless barbarians from invading. The feudalistic teachings of Buddhism taught that people's duty in life was simply to submit to their masters. This kept peasants from trying to improve their conditions. They were also plagued by tuberculosis, malaria, rheumatic fever, and malnutrition. My grandfather died of rheumatic fever when I was a boy. There was little that could be done to help him."

"What about the traditional doctors?" I asked. "Didn't they help?"

Dr. Cheng perked up. "Oh, we are very proud of them, even today. With herbs and roots and acupuncture they could often help chronic ailments, but could not do much for acute diseases. It wasn't until the 1840s that western doctors first came and taught our people to take better care of themselves. The American Church Mission built a string of hospitals extending from Shanghai to Nan Jing, 150 miles away. These doctors were some of the first to come to China."

At this, we came across the hospital barber shop. Here stood two old barber chairs and a line of men waiting to be trimmed. The music of an oriental violin and gong came from a transistor radio, giving the room an antique feel. Approaching the door, I was amazed to find that the hinges read, "London, England."

Dr. Cheng noticed my gaze. "You're probably wondering how those hinges got here. A British dentist by the name of Henry Lester came here in 1846 and built this hospital. The people in England sent a great deal of money and supplies. Perhaps more important, many of their doctors and nurses traveled here and died serving my people."

I thought, *These people must have gone through a lot more than I to come here. I wonder what motivated them?* I decided to ask.

"Let me ask you something, Dr. Cheng. You have said that life in those times was very hard. Why do you think these people left the comforts of England, risked six months in a ship at sea, and learned to speak Chinese just to work in this hospital?"

Dr. Cheng scratched his head. "Good question! I don't know exactly why it was, but one thing I do know. Many of them were Christians. You see that building over there?" He pointed out a window to a rather dilapidated structure. "A church met there at one time, but now it is used for political education."

I wondered just what he meant by "political education," but decided it might be too sensitive a question to ask. "Where did the hospital's name come from?" I asked.

"Initially, it was called the Charity Hospital, but that name is a reminder of the Christian way of thought. We Marxists have a better way today, better than the Christians, better than the Buddhists. So, during the Cultural Revolution the name was changed to the Third People's Hospital. This was to tell us that the hospital and its work belongs to all of us."

As the two of us walked on, I saw a sign with the letters

"OPD" above it. I reasoned that perhaps this meant "Out Patient Department." We entered an auditorium filled with people who stood around rugged desks. Each of the patients had a chart in hand and stood waiting for the attention of the consultant seated before him. The rattling and honking of trucks, the clang of bicycle bells, and the shouting of people outside came through the open windows of the sweltering hot clinic. Vainly, now and again, a doctor tried to listen to someone's heartbeat, but it must have been difficult to distinguish from the rhythm of a nearby pile driver.

"Every day in this outpatient clinic we see thousands of people for their high blood pressure, diabetes, pneumonia, and colds. The facilities are not plush like yours in America, but we do perform quite well with only the basic equipment. A doctor's mind is far more important than his instruments." Dr. Cheng shouted to make himself heard above the noise. "One of the virtues we value most is simplicity. These doctors have learned to get by with just the essentials. Let's keep moving."

Just outside the clinic we passed a lean-to next to the main building filled with several large baskets overflowing with surgical gloves, rubber tubing, needles, and syringes. In some others were thrown drapes, gowns, and blankets. The emblem on one of the blankets caught my eye. It read in bold letters "Property of the U.S. Navy." I wondered how it got there. Dr. Cheng must have guessed my next question.

"That blanket was probably exchanged by some American sailor in port for gifts he wanted to buy. There were a lot of them here after the Japanese left."

"In the United States most of these needles and syringes would be used once and then thrown away," I commented.

"But not so here," said Dr. Cheng. "True, it is an inconvenience to wash and re-sterilize this equipment, but it's much less expensive to do so. Also, our staff takes better care not to damage these things, knowing that they will be used many times. We even have workers whose job it is to sharpen the needle points with a file."

Next we entered a cellar filled with many fragrant aromas. It was the traditional medicine pharmacy. On dozens of shelves were drawers, each containing a particular stalk, root, or leaf. In the center sat an official-looking person with a scale in hand. She was rather like a librarian, said Dr. Cheng; she guided doctors to the proper remedy. He introduced me, and I asked her what sort of training was required to do her job.

She said that she had received four years of instruction beyond medical school that qualified her to prescribe these drugs. "Often our people do not trust the drugs from western countries," she said. "They are too powerful and harsh. We prefer to use drugs that are more gentle and that have been used and tested for hundreds of years before approving them. Their actions are slow and more natural. You will learn a lot about them while you are here."

I thought that sometimes our Food and Drug Administration also tested drugs over hundreds of years before approving them! As we left the room, I asked Dr. Cheng how they distinguished a "traditional medicine" from other types of drugs.

He grinned widely. "If it might help and can't hurt, it's a traditional medicine." He chuckled. "Actually, we are not purists. We use a combination of Western and Chinese therapies now. Even Mao Tse-tung encouraged this."

The sun had begun to set and we walked out onto a balcony to watch. Soot hung over the city, enveloping it like a dark cloud. Factory employees streamed into the boulevards on their bicycles, and street vendors were closing up their shops. Ending our excursion, Dr. Cheng challenged me.

"I want you to criticize us and correct our doctors whenever something is wrong. We want to learn from you and expect you to teach us about American medical practice. You have a lot of knowledge to share with us. But this will be a true exchange. We will also give you ideas about life that may enlighten you. We have found the solution to the greatest problems of society."

This speech caught me off-guard. How was I going to be their teacher? I was only twenty-four and quite a rookie doctor, yet they expected big things from me. And what were these "ideas" and "solutions" he mentioned?

What had I gotten myself into? What lay ahead I could not predict.

Several days later, I stood outside the cardiology depart-ment waiting for the arrival of Dr. Tao, whom I had met earlier. He had been assigned to be my guide and professor while I was in China. I preferred to wait for him to introduce me to the other doctors inside, for I had heard that this was the custom. I had quickly given up on the suit and tie and had bought some shorts and a shirt like the ones Dr. Cheng wore. It was almost unavoidable that I should overhear the conversation coming from the doctors within.

"What? There is an American going to work with us?" said one surprised doctor. "Why would he want to come here?"

"He must have an ulterior motive," replied another. "Perhaps he is a spy or from the CIA and wants to find out our country's weaknesses. I would be careful around him. Don't say too much!"

"Or he could be a fugitive running from the police in America—or maybe from his girlfriend," said a third, laughing.

"This is remarkable," I thought. "The Americans can't see why I'd want to leave, and the Chinese can't comprehend why I'd want to come." Their suspicion made me uneasy.

They continued. "I wonder what it is like in America? It sounds wonderful. I've heard that some people even make more than $6,000 a year! That's ten times as much as I make."

"And there is every kind of freedom there. A person can even change jobs without approval from the authorities."

"How can that be? I don't believe it could be so easy."

"But it's true. I heard about it on the radio from Hong Kong. Still, there are some things that I don't understand. Like why did the Americans try to establish those colonies in Korea and Vietnam? They sent so many soldiers there. They must be very greedy. Also, why do they keep Chinese slaves to work the factories in Hong Kong?"

"The *China Daily* also says that Americans can keep their own guns in their homes, without even a permit. And I've read that many people shoot one another for almost no reason. I don't think that it is safe in America. Here no one ever gets shot. They have too much freedom!" Several others agreed.

Maybe he is right about that one! I thought.

Then another spoke up. "I also understand that many men and women live with one another, but are not married. Some of them have children, who are then raised by only their mother. This is a shameful thing! It's almost unheard of for this to happen in China. Marriage is an honorable thing here, much better than going from woman to woman. Americans don't seem to realize this. They must be afraid of close relationships. We do not need their influence here!"

Then the man who started the discussion broke in. "I have been told by the hospital authorities not to talk with him. We need to be careful until we know what he is up to."

Just then, Dr. Tao arrived. We walked into the ward together to discuss the condition of our critical patients, the first order of business for the day. The men immediately dropped their conversation and straightened up as if caught with their pants down. They eyed me curiously.

Dr. Tao noticed that they felt uneasy at our sudden entry and said, "Sorry to interrupt your conversation. What were you talking about?"

After a brief pause and some anxious looks among them, one man answered, "The volleyball game. We were talking about the volleyball game."

Dr. Tao looked satisfied and walked to the first bedside. He took his position of authority immediately on the patient's right side, while the young doctors formed a semicircle about them. He glanced at us to assure complete attention. Then he opened his mouth and began to utter the most unintelligible speech I had ever heard. All around me the young men and women scribbled down notes and seemed to comprehend entirely this alien jargon. I stood there for several minutes like an invalid. When I could stand it no longer, I blurted out, "Wait. What are you saying?"

Stopping abruptly, Dr. Tao gazed at me with a thoughtful eye. Then he smiled. "Oh, I'm sorry, Dr. Kong, you cannot understand. I was talking in the Shanghai dialect." I looked at him curiously, and he explained. "This is our own language. In southern China each major city or province has its own local language. If you travel fifty miles from Shanghai, you'll find that they speak an almost entirely different language from ours. This situation, of course, is hard for people like you, but it is hard for us as well. It causes great problems in communication throughout the nation. In the schools, however, we are all taught to speak Mandarin, as you speak. It is the standard language here. Still, many older persons in

China can not speak Mandarin. In the future I'll try to remember you can't understand our own dialect."

I noticed later that the Mandarin of some Shanghai doctors was not much better than my own, for they spoke the Shanghai dialect most of the time.

We visited several patients during that hour before we came to the last for the day. It was Li Ming, the patient with the infected heart, who had been carried in from the field by his friends. Now, a few days later, he was conscious but still weak. His wife sat at his bedside, mopping the sweat from his brow. Li was a well-built man, but he looked up at us with an expression of utter fatigue. In spite of his poor condition, he possessed a glimmer of confidence I couldn't quite understand.

Li's infected heart continued to beat poorly. The night before, his blood pressure had become dangerously low and his heart rhythm was irregular. He had received the best drugs I could think of, but he needed something more. As we were discussing his treatment, I asked Dr. Tao for advice.

Dr. Tao slowly drew from his pocket two long needles and an alcohol swab. Taking hold of Li's wrist, he made a mark on his wrist, close to the thumb. Here he thrust in a needle about one inch deep, then repeated the procedure on the opposite wrist. Li seemed pleased with the two new needles piercing his skin.

"In traditional Chinese medicine," Dr. Tao said, "we call this point 'neiguan.' It has been discovered that by stimulating this area with a needle, the strength of the heart contraction is increased temporarily."

"Fascinating," I said. "How does it work?"

"We don't understand the mechanism of how it works, only that it usually does. This area that I punctured has no relationship to any major arteries or nerves. Be sure to come by later and tell me whether he improves."

We broke up to see the rest of the patients on our own. The first one I was to see was Su Ping, who had just been admitted. During our rounds, I had been assigned to his care. When I approached his bed, there appeared to be only a large pile of blankets on it. I could not tell whether he was there or not. I deduced that either he was an extremely small boy, or he was indeed not under them. I looked under the blankets without success, so I continued my search elsewhere.

The day was beastly hot and every window was open to catch the occasional breeze. Suddenly a gust of wind blew through the ward, bringing a cloud of coal dust from the factory next door. The black powder began to settle on all the furnishings and people. The patients who were able quickly jumped up to close the windows. Others began coughing and sputtering. I was worried that we might have several persons with breathing trouble. The doors leading to the balcony burst open and in came several others who had been sitting outside. They, too, were escaping the dust. Among them was the boy, Su Ping, carried by his father.

His round purple face greeted me apathetically. The boy's thin, ghostly hands clung to his father. His first problem was obvious: a gigantic, fluid-filled abdomen. Back inside the ward I asked his father to explain to me how this illness had begun, but he did not answer me a word. I thought this very strange. How did he expect to get any help without talking? I asked him again to please talk to me. Then I noticed that he seemed to be scared.

"I have been told before not to speak with foreigners," he said.

"But I am your son's doctor! I am here to help you. You can make an exception this time. Do not worry!"

He seemed a little consoled. As a child, he said, Su Ping had slowly become more and more fatigued. By the time he was seven years old he preferred to sit inside their cool home made of rocks and mud rather than play outside. He continued to grow worse in spite of care from several doctors in the countryside. Finally, when he was no longer able to walk, his family brought him the one thousand miles by train to Shanghai. We were their last hope of finding a cure.

I examined the pathetic figure. *Why is it,* I thought, as I often had before, *that little children can become so sick?*

His father then perked up as if he had an idea. He said to me, "You know that my son's situation is so terrible. There seems to be nothing more that the physicians here can do. But surely you know of some cure from America that we can use." His expression was forlorn and appealing. He added, "The United States has the very best doctors, and I know that you can help us."

Well, his attitude has changed toward me now! I thought. I confessed to him that I did not know exactly what had caused Su's condition, but that it certainly had to do with his heart. We would do our best to discover the problem and care for him.

Perhaps there was no cure for Su Ping. Maybe all of his father's efforts were in vain. Yet, the worst thing I could do would be to talk away all hope from him.

The father walked slowly to his son's side. He picked up a halved watermelon. With a spoon he dug into the melon and dropped the fruit into Su's open mouth. Then he embraced Su in a warm hug.

I left the two of them alone and walked toward Li Ming's bed. At that moment a startled nurse was taking Li's blood pressure.

"What is it?" I asked.

"It has come back to normal now. Amazing!" she said with a smile. Li Ming grinned also. I noticed that confident air about him again. He reached for a bamboo fan at his bedside and began to fan himself.

His nurse removed the blood pressure cuff from his arm and the thermometer from his mouth. She then picked up the cuff to move on to the other patients. Before her lay a row of patients who already had thermometers in their mouths. In a moment she would walk by each and read their temperatures. Our eyes fell on one man who reached up and took the thermometer from his mouth. He rested its silver tip on the mattress cover and began rubbing the thermometer vigorously. After a moment, he straightened up and read the temperature. Not high enough, he must have decided. He continued to rub for another minute before returning it to his mouth. Did anyone see him? He glanced around. Apparently not. He settled back on his pillow, his face smooth and innocent.

The nurse and I looked at one another as if to say, "Did you see that?"

"He is just doing that so that he won't have to go back to work," she said with disgust. Still, I thought I could see a smile breaking between her lips.

"But what would he be doing for income while he is here?" I asked.

"Workers get paid the same regardless of whether they are in the hospital or not," she said. "Here they are cared for and the food is good. What a coward! It's time for us to have a talk." She turned from me and marched toward his bed, fuming.

I remembered that Dr. Cheng had asked me to see him that day, so I started off toward his office down on the first floor. He had an attractive secretary in front, who announced my arrival and showed me in. He met me at the door in his usual warm manner and motioned me toward a chair.

"Well, Dr. Kong, how has your stay in China been so far? Have you felt welcomed by the people here?"

"On the whole I have," I replied. "Your staff has been very courteous to me. I believe that they find me to be a constant topic of conversation." I grinned.

"That you are! Your arrival is perhaps the most remarkable thing that has happened here in over a year."

"I have sensed that many people are reluctant to talk to me. They seem to be afraid. Why is this?"

Dr. Cheng smiled. "Our people are wary of any bad influences that they might pick up from foreigners. This is why they are careful around you. Just give it time, and they will warm up to you."

"Bad influences?" I asked, feeling like I might be contaminating something. "What bad influences?"

"Oh, people from America are known for drinking in excess, fighting with one another, shooting each other, and things like that. We are forming a new type of society here in China: one that is free of these evils, one where people work for the good of the community. So, you see, we are careful to screen out any contrary ideas."

My ears perked up. Here was someone who was interested in the same things as I was. "Tell me more about this society of yours, Dr. Cheng."

"We are Marxists in China." Dr. Cheng settled himself comfortably into his chair. "We have set ourselves to overcome the social injustices that have persisted for centuries—in particular, the wide discrepancies between the rich and poor, and the selfishness that is so common in the West."

"I'm impressed that you are confronting these important

issues. So many others simply gloss over these problems as unsolvable."

Dr. Cheng gave me a solemn look. "But, Dr. Kong, we are not even close to this end. It will take a long time to reach it."

At that moment Dr. Tao put his head in at the door. "Dr. Kong, I have been looking for you, but I see that you are in good hands. We are late for the clinic." He looked at Dr. Cheng, who returned a nod of approval.

"I'd like to know more about how your country is trying to change people for the better," I said as we walked out of the room.

"That we will leave to another day," Dr. Cheng promised.

Dr. Tao and I made our way down to the open hall of the clinic and took a seat at one of the desks. Before us was a hard examining table and a sea of round faces, waiting in line to be seen.

The first patient was a middle-aged woman, puffing for breath and walking slowly. She sat down with some difficulty and said that it was becoming more and more hard for her to breathe. She had sought relief with a number of herbal remedies, but to no avail. In the awful heat of summer things were even worse.

I asked her to lie down on the hard, wood examining table next to us. As she did, her breathing became even more labored, so I examined her quickly. The great veins of her neck were protruding. Her lungs sounded wet with fluid. When I listened to her heart, I heard a roaring murmur, which told me the key to her problem. She was gasping for breath now, so Dr. Tao and I pulled her bolt upright.

"It's really nothing," she said as soon as she could manage a word. "I'll be all right after a moment."

"Actually, you have a serious problem with one of your heart valves," I said. "It won't go away in a moment. But I believe that we can help you. It would be best if you would stay in the hospital for a few days." Dr. Tao nodded his agreement.

"Oh, doctor, I believe I can manage. I just have a little flu," she said between puffs. "Can't I just keep on taking these medicines and wait for a while? I don't like hospitals."

The little crowd of waiting patients standing behind now had their eyes fixed on us.

"You can hardly stand up, let alone walk home," I said. "Look at yourself heaving. You should not put this off any longer."

Still, she protested violently. The thought of being dependent on someone else to help her must have insulted her pride. When she continued to object, Dr. Tao leaned close to the lady's ear and spoke most persuasively.

"This is Dr. Kong. He is an American and quite a specialist in his field. In fact, he came here just to help people with your disease. If he thinks you need to enter the hospital, you can be sure that his conclusion is correct and the best that we can offer you."

"Oh, an American." She shot me a glance. "I thought that he was Russian. And good, right? Well, if that's the case, then I'd better follow his advice."

Dr. Tao drew back, obviously impressed with the success of this tactical approach. Later, I reminded him that I was not a specialist in cardiology. Still, throughout the year I was often conveniently referred to as a specialist in many different areas. It was quite amusing to be credited with such a wealth of knowledge.

Because of my status as resident foreign "expert," I was asked to give my opinions at the medical conferences held each week. This was the big meeting of the hospital staff and it seemed to have several unwritten rules about it. The meeting room would fill, first with medical students in the back row, bashful lest anyone should pose a question to them. Next came the resident doctors, confident but quiet in deference to the professors, who occupied the front rows. A lone intern would stand and rapidly read the history of the sick person being considered that day, then dive to the back of the room to avoid cross-examination. Following this, a few professors would stand and briefly state their judgments regarding the case. Some of the professors, who enjoyed the satisfaction of a captive audience, often continued for some time. This caused most students to conclude that brevity was indeed a virtue absent from our discussions. I often spent the time reviewing my Chinese vocabulary from a small notebook that I carried.

Finally, to give the last word, the most elder professor would explain his views, commonly referring to advanced concepts gleaned from American medical journals. I was continually impressed by their knowledge. Although Chinese facilities were still in the Dark Ages, their knowledge was quite up-to-date.

On one occasion, as Dr. Cheng was speaking, I was struck by his features. In comparison to his body, his head was rather large. A dominant forehead sloped down from his balding scalp, but most impressive were his long, almost elephantlike ears, which swayed at the side of his head when he turned.

I nudged Dr. Tao sitting next to me. "Look at his ears!"

"Oh. Uh? What?" I must have awakened him.

"Dr. Cheng's ears—see how large they are!"

Dr. Tao gazed casually a moment and then whispered to me. "Well, of course! You have much to learn, Kong. Long ears are a sign of a long, prosperous life. A large head means the same thing. This is a well-known fact in China. Even from childhood you can tell the span of a person's life by these signs. Just look at the other professors."

My eyes moved up and down the long row of gray-haired men up front. Sure enough, their ears stood out proudly. Dr. Tao leaned close. "Kong, how large are your ears?"

I was afraid to look.

As the weeks went by it became clear that the frail boy, Su Ping, was progressively worsening. I was really worried about him. I went to his bed first each morning and held his weak hand. "How are you feeling?" I would ask. Often, there was no voiced reply, only an expression of helplessness that made my heart sink. He could no longer sit up, and an infusion of medication was required almost constantly to keep his heart beating. A special instrument, the ultrasound, which operates rather like a sonar beam on ships, had detected a large mass in the boy's heart.

In order to identify what this mass was we needed to examine a piece of it. This meant a dangerous procedure, made even worse by Su's poor condition. Still, he'd certainly die if we did not do something.

Su was taken to the operating room and carefully put to sleep. We then made an incision into a vein in his neck and passed some long forceps through the vein and down into the inside of his heart to take out a piece of the mass. The incision was then closed and Su was taken back to the ward. Later, the pathologist reported that the mass was cancer of the heart muscle, a very rare disease with no known cure. We could only offer to support him as long as possible. Painfully aware of the prognosis, Su's father was more concerned about his son's agony, sleepless nights, and constant abdominal pain.

One afternoon I found him kneeling outside the ward,

eyeing his son through the doorway. He held a cigarette. As I walked by, he motioned me near.

"What is the use of all this?" he said, standing and pointing toward the bed. "My son is going to die. Why should you keep trying to help him? All you are doing is prolonging his agony. You are the one making him suffer!" His cigarette dropped to the floor and his fists clenched. "Stop the medicine and let him die!" He grabbed my coat collar and wrenched it up tight.

I stood still, not daring to move. He was a big man for a Chinese. A clerk stopped short down the hall to watch the drama. Su's father let out a whimper, then a soft cry as he released me. Tears ran down his face. "It is so hard!" he cried. "I have gone to the Buddha so many times! I've spent days on my stomach in the temple, pleading for my son's life. My wife, she has sold almost all that we own to bring the money as sacrifices to Buddha's altar." He eased back down onto his knees. "But the Buddha does not listen. He is deaf. He is only stone and he has taken my last hope away."

"Daddy!" A voice rang out into the hall. "Daddy, where are you?" It was Su Ping.

At first the man seemed to ignore the call. Then he shook himself. Like a flash he jolted up. His wrinkled forehead smoothed out and he trotted into the ward. I straightened out my shirt and gave a sigh of relief. Perhaps he still had some hope left.

Several days later I was back in the weekly outpatient clinic seeing a host of children suffering from congenital heart defects. Most were very small for their age and often had purple lips and fingers. These children came to the Third People's Hospital from all over China, for it was one of the few places where corrective heart surgery could be performed. Without this care many of their little lives would be cut short. As I finished admitting one little girl to the hospital in the late afternoon, Dr. Tao called me over to his desk on the adult side of the clinic.

"Dr. Kong, this woman has been ill for several days. I want to know what you think. She has had a fever of 101 degrees, a cough, and a runny nose. She also has been sneezing quite a lot. Her little girl, here, also has the same thing."

"Sounds like a cold to me," I replied. It seemed simple enough.

"Yes, and how would you treat this in America?" asked Tao, probing.

"I'd tell her to rest at home and drink plenty of fluids. I might also prescribe an antihistamine-decongestant to help the symptoms."

Dr. Tao shook his head. "Come, come, Kong. You know that those medicines don't really help. In China we have something much better." He opened a drawer and pulled out a bottle filled with a black shiny fluid. Pouring a small amount into a teaspoon, he lifted it to the woman's lips. "This formula is made from snake gall bladders!" he announced. "A certain cure for any cold. One dose does it!" The spoon dropped into her mouth and she swallowed the potion straightaway. I could not help but gag at the thought.

Next in line came a man clutching his chest and leaning on a cane. His appearance was strikingly more Caucasian than the others in the room, and his speech was very difficult to understand. A nurse went in search of an interpreter for us, and we soon learned that he was from a northern province of China, near Russia. He talked for several minutes quite vividly, swinging his arms about for expression.

"What is he saying?" I asked Dr. Tao.

"Dr. Kong, this man says that he has had crushing chest pains for ten years, that he never urinates, and that his heart stops beating for minutes at a time. What do you think of his diagnosis?"

I detected a smile hovering on Dr. Tao's lips. "Neurosis, sir," I replied.

"Right you are!" He clapped his hands together. Then he reached into his coat pocket and pulled out a small envelope. "As a reward I have a ticket for you to go to the sports arena tonight, compliments of Dr. Cheng. You must have seen some patients like this in America!"

"Lots and lots!" I replied.

At the end of the day I shed my large lab coat and hung it on a peg in the office I shared with several other doctors. The black, single-speed bicycle that I used to ride to work stood outside along the street, with hundreds of others like it. Though private cars were not allowed, bicycles were plentiful and could be bought for the equivalent of three months' wages. A pink receipt had been given to me by an attendant that morning when I parked it. She had locks of gray hair curled about her shoulders and a smock with coins that rattled about as she walked.

"Dr. Kong, are you going out to play now?" she asked, receiving my ticket. This was a very popular expression. It was used even by the most elderly to describe their recreation.

I hopped aboard my bicycle. "Yes, I'm off to see the NBA All-Star team from America play basketball with your Nan Jing Army. Should be an exciting night!"

"Oh, the Americans will have a tough time against our men," she said. "They are the very best. The radio has been talking about them all day! They are from the People's Liberation Army. They overthrew the Japanese, chased out the Nationalists, and now the Americans are next!" She talked as if she meant it.

"We shall see," I said, and waved to her as I rode off. I wound my way through the myriad of other cyclists on the street. Now and then a car came honking past us, but they were persistently ignored by the cyclists. The weather began to turn cool as I rode along, and the overcast clouds above appeared threatening. Soon rain began to fall, first in droplets, then in a torrent. Hardly inhibited, the others rode on in their raincoats. I followed suit, putting on the coat that I carried on the rack in back of my bike, but the wind blew the water straight into my face. So I pulled my umbrella from the carrying rack over the back wheel and held it overhead with one hand as I pedaled. This helped quite a bit.

Shortly afterward, an elderly man glided up beside me.

"You can't do that!" he said in a gruff voice.

"Do what?" came my innocent reply.

"It's against the law to ride with only one hand on the handlebars. It's too dangerous!"

I had never heard of this before, but I took his advice and folded up the umbrella. Back came the flood into my face. Still, I could make out another bicyclist about thirty yards ahead who also was holding up an umbrella, so I watched him closely. An electric trolley beside him suddenly pulled out in front. I saw the man's umbrella fall as he grabbed for the handle brakes. Too late! Down went the bike into a gutter filled with rushing water. As I pulled to a stop, he stood up. It seemed that only his pride was hurt. Some bystanders were laughing, and the trolley moved on its way. I could not help but have empathy for him. It could have been me.

After I dried myself off and had dinner, I headed for the Shanghai Sports Arena, where the game was to be held. When I arrived the arena was already crowded to overflowing with thousands of eager Chinese. They bustled about the halls of the new building, talking excitedly. When I walked out into the open seating area, I stood still to look around. After a moment of looking for a place to sit, I spotted some Westerners sitting a few rows over. I immediately went over to them.

"Hello!" I said, approaching a sandy-haired young man.

"Well, hello to you, too," he said as he turned. "I did not know that there were any other Americans here."

"You are the first one I have met in Shanghai, aside from those at the Consulate. My name is Kong—I mean, Comninellis, Nicholas Comninellis."

"And I am Keith Johnson. We're all language students at the Shanghai Teachers College." He began to introduce me to a half a dozen others in the group. As he did so, I felt a twinge of homesickness.

Then the announcer walked out on the court to give the introductions. He said something about promoting international friendship and the like. We watched intently as the players were introduced. The Army team was dressed in green uniforms and led by a center barely six feet tall. Their warm-up brought peals of applause from the fans. Next up, the comparative giants of the NBA were greeted by near silence. Only some hissing was heard when the black players, who were the majority, were presented. It was the first time I encountered Chinese prejudice toward black people, though not the last.

The ball was tipped off and the spectators roared with excitement. An Army man had the first drive downcourt. He dodged the defense and laid the ball up for the first two points. The crowd went wild. They pounded their feet and we thought the roof might cave in. An American player snatched the ball and threw it toward the Army's goal. At half-court another caught the ball and suddenly stopped short. He launched it into the air. The arena went silent as the ball fell, penetrating the basket with a swish that echoed about the great pillars. Not a soul applauded.

The Army scooped up the ball and again ran down court. With perfect coordination, an Army player shot the ball between the legs of a rival and another sank it in for two more points. The Chinese roared with delight. The All-Stars seemed impressed at the Army's teamwork. They regrouped and worked the ball quickly back to shooting range and connected the basket with another loud swish against a background of silence.

I noticed that there was a definite pattern developing. We could not just keep quiet! Our small band of Americans decided that the time had come for action. We huddled amid the screaming masses and decided on some chants and songs we'd learned in college. Then, during the silence that followed a score for the neglected team, we filled the air with cheers of encouragement. Seven of us versus thousands of Chinese. More than once an American player shouted out his approval of the boisterous Americans who urged them on. Our sideline performance even caused some Chinese spectators to join in.

By the end of the fourth quarter the score was irrelevant. Together, both Chinese and Americans had had fun and knew one another better than before, just as the announcer had said. International brotherhood was advanced, cultural exchange accomplished, but I still felt some patriotic pride—for the American team had thoroughly beaten the Army!

When I returned to the hospital the next morning, I found Su Ping's father waiting, balanced on his haunches, by the front gate. He rose slowly when I walked up. Not a word did he offer, only an expressionless stare that I had not seen from him before. I could only speculate about what had happened as I walked to the ward.

When I arrived, a nurse took me aside and said, "Ta suh-da." I did not know what she meant until I went to Su's bed. There, Su lay quiet, covered with a clean sheet. His years of struggle had ended. A young doctor began to speculate about the final cause of death, but another motioned him to silence as we stood quietly for a moment to respect our departed friend. I felt sick to my stomach. This poor child never knew the joy of playing outside or jumping a rope. I thought of my sister who was just his age—it might have been her instead of him—and I felt even worse.

Li Ming, who had now been in the hospital for two months, noticed my poorly camouflaged grief. He called me over to him and I walked to his bedside.

"Come now, it is all right to cry, Dr. Kong," he said.

"It was difficult to see him die little by little," I explained. "Even though I knew that there was little we could do to help him, still it saddens me when the inevitable happens. It's not that I feel I have failed. It is something deeper than that."

Li looked intently at the covered figure across the room and listened a moment to the muffled conversations about us. "Dr. Kong, I know what it is. You are first a human, not a physician or some godlike character. You are saddened over the loss of a friend. You did not know him well, but you did spend a lot of time with him this summer. You have lost a companion. It is good that you experience these feelings. More dangerous it would be by far if you were immune to the suffering of the people who need your help.

"You see, many of the atrocities of our world are committed by people who have lost regard for the turmoil of others. They are more interested in their own satisfaction. The sad fact of it all is that so few people ever realize that the deepest satisfaction and happiness comes not from seeking to please themselves. It comes from helping to meet the needs of other people. Keep up your work, Kong. It's not in vain."

I knew that he must be right.

chapter three

Reeducation

D R. TAO AND I WERE ENCOURAGED. There was no doubt about it: Li Ming was gradually improving. As the weeks went by, his heart beat more regularly and the fluid left his lungs. First, he was able to be up out of bed for a few minutes at a time, then fatigue would overtake him; but as the summer closed, he went about the ward doing the most remarkable things. I came in one morning to find him at a sink with a dozen pair of pants. He was scrubbing them meticulously clean with his bare hands.

A nurse took me aside. "Li is so much better. He has not stopped going today! He went from bed to bed this morning asking the other patients if he could wash their clothes. He did not even ask to be paid in return. What's more, look at his smile. It's contagious!"

"I've also noticed his cheerful attitude. Why is he so different from the other people here?" I asked, looking at the solemn faces of the staff working around us.

"I don't really know. Perhaps it has something to do with that book I see him reading occasionally."

Dr. Tao came up beside me and we looked at Li from across the room. "Kong, it gives me hope when I see someone like him recover. I don't know just how much of it was anything we did. Still, he could relapse any time. I'd like to give him a checkup in a few weeks. Let's let him go home for now."

I was happy with Dr. Tao's decision and went over to tell Li. He was deep in conversation with another man when I approached, so I waited a moment.

"It's easy to be kind when things are easy and good," he was saying. "The test is in the hard times. When we realize that we are loved, then we can be fulfilled and have the desire to help other people. That's the secret."

As I listened, a thought occurred to me: *I wonder if he is also a Marxist, like Dr. Cheng. He certainly seems to have some virtues.* Then Li turned toward me.

"Oh, Dr. Kong, how are you today?" His face was bright, though still a little thin.

"Very well, and even better since I heard the news."

"What is that?"

"You are doing so well now that we want to discharge you today."

His face became even brighter. "That would be wonderful! It has been so long since I've been home. Thank you, Dr. Kong. You have helped me so much." His countenance suddenly changed, as if he remembered something. "I want to show you how grateful I am!"

He went to his bedside and opened a small drawer in the cabinet next to it. In the drawer lay a white porcelain mug with a floral pattern hand-painted on the side. He held it up in both palms and then handed it to me. "Dr. Kong, I want you to live long and have a prosperous life! Please accept this gift from me and use it in your home across the ocean."

I admired the beautiful mug, thanked him, and placed it into my coat pocket. I was finished with my work for the morning, so I said, "I'd be honored to walk with you to the train station."

He agreed, and after he packed his few belongings into an old rice sack, we made our way out to the street.

As we walked outside, I noticed a young man and woman walking arm in arm in front of us. Her black hair was lightly curled and her features were quite attractive. Li Ming noticed the couple also and spoke up. "Dr. Kong, do you know what the love ducks are?"

"No, I haven't heard of them," I replied.

"In our tradition the mandarin ducks are a symbol of marriage. This is because the two of them are always side by side in the water. One never leaves the other. They are a symbol of love and commitment."

Just then the woman lifted her chin and cleared her throat loudly. Then she turned her head to the side and spit forcefully into the gutter.

"But that," continued Li, "is a tradition we could do without." I agreed with him. There were several others on the sidewalk with us who spat as they went along.

We stopped a moment on a corner where a man was selling his wares, something in a large boiling vat. A propane bottle stood nearby to feed the flames. He took the wooden lid off the top to serve someone. Inside were steaming dumplings, perfect for the cool afternoon. I placed an order for us, my mouth watering as he piled the dumplings into two paper dishes. We took them with us to eat along the way. Inside each round ball of bread was a piece of pork that tasted heavenly.

The street was quite rough where we were walking. I was startled by a loaded bicycle that sped by.

"Look at them go!" I exclaimed.

"It's an entire family," said Li. "Look. The one over the peddles is the husband. His wife is sitting on the back fender with a baby in her lap, and on the handlebar seat is their boy. Quite ingenious!"

The bike shook a little and swayed from side to side as they rolled on.

Li continued, "That man has a bamboo stick in his lung."

"A what?"

"He has a bamboo stick in his lung. Oh, you don't understand. It's an expression we use. It means that he has confidence. I'd never be able to ride four on a bike. In fact, in my village there are hardly any bikes at all! It is a very simple place with only a single dirt road. There is a range of mountains in the distance and a small river that winds through the center. So pretty! In the evenings there is a purple haze over the rice fields and you can hear the call of birds. We Chinese have a dear love for our hometowns. It's hard to explain, but I'll be there soon."

Now we were coming to the entrance of the train station, marked by a large neon sign in Chinese characters. Li Ming seemed to know where he was going, so I followed him into the huge station. It was rather like an airplane hangar, with a steel superstructure overhead. We got into a long line to buy a ticket.

"You will get a true taste of China here, Dr. Kong," said Li. He was looking into the terminal waiting room. There, on wooden benches dozens of yards long, was a sea of humanity seated side by side. A platoon of soldiers from the People's Liberation Army stood nearby, easily distinguished by the red rectangles on their collars. Behind them were several families walking along the corridor with their bundles. Some balanced long poles across their shoulders to ease the burden of the sack of possessions hung from each end.

Next to us I noticed a woman who was crying over her small baby. Great tears were rolling down her face. Li lost no time in going right over to her. "What is the problem?" he said gently.

"I just don't know what to do," she sobbed. "We're traveling to Wu Nan tonight to join my husband, but after I bought our ticket there was no money left. Now my baby has begun to cry. She has not eaten since yesterday. I have nothing to give her!" She burst into tears again.

Li Ming looked touched. He spoke to her a moment and then disappeared from the station. I wondered what he was up to. Most Chinese I knew were rather distant with strangers. They were not likely to get involved with matters not their own business, but not Li!

A few minutes later he returned with two jars of milk in one hand and a loaf of bread in the other. He was beaming again and gave them to the woman. She cried out with joy. Immediately she fed the milk to the baby, who gulped it down frantically.

Li and I had just rejoined our long line to buy his ticket when a well-dressed official walked up to us.

"It's not necessary for you to wait in line, sir," he said to me. "You are a foreigner. We have a special ticket office for you. Follow me." He immediately led us into an ornate lobby with plush carpet and couches. Potted trees circled the desk where he seated himself.

"I am with the China Travel Bureau," he said to me. "We want to make your vacation here a pleasant one. Now, where would you like to go?"

"Actually, I'm not the one traveling. It's my friend who is taking the train," I said, turning to Li.

"Oh, well, I'm sorry. I did not understand." The officer frowned. "He'll have to go back and stand in line with the others." He stood up to dismiss us.

"Wait a minute. You brought us here. Now you're going to put him out? That's not right!"

"That's our policy here. A common man does not qualify for our services. Only foreign guests do."

"We have lost our place in line. I insist that you give him his ticket, or else I'll find your superior."

The official backed down. "Well, I suppose we can accommodate you." He turned to Li Ming. "Let me see your identification card, your work unit number, your rice coupons, and your travel permit."

"I don't have any of these with me," said Li, sitting on the edge of his seat.

The man frowned again. "Well, I certainly can't issue you a ticket. In fact, I should report you to the police for traveling as a vagrant without a permit." He reached for the phone. Then he looked up again. "Besides, you know that it's against the law to associate with a foreign guest."

"Wait a moment," said Li, calm but pressing. "You see, I was brought to Shanghai from my village when I was very ill. There was no way I could bring my cards with me. Now I've been released from the hospital. I need to get back home."

"A likely story!" He continued to dial the phone. "Hello, police? I have a vagrant here that must be taken away. No . . . he does not have any papers."

Meanwhile, I was stewing in my seat with righteous anger. I couldn't keep quiet any longer. "Everything Li Ming says is true! I can vouch for it. I am his doctor!" I said, laying my identification on the desk. "We are from the Third People's Hospital."

The official looked surprised. He spoke quietly into the receiver and then hung up. "Hum." He scratched his chin. "I see that you are. I've never heard of a foreign doctor working here before." He let out a sigh. "I won't trouble you any further." He reached into a drawer and drew out a train ticket. He stamped it and presented it to Li. Then he bowed. "Have a pleasant trip."

Li replied sincerely, "I'm sorry to have troubled you!"

We walked out on the loading platform and looked over the train before departure. Coal was being loaded into the steam locomotive. I noticed that a few of the cars in front were quite plush, with velvet seats and tea tables. The others were drab, with hard wood benches, and had a foul smell. "Who gets to ride in those cars up there?" I asked Li.

"Oh, those are for foreign visitors," he said.

"Does anyone else get to sit there?" I inquired.

"Yes. Also Communist Party members." He did not seem to be much concerned about this.

"Li," I said, "are you a member of the Party?"

He looked surprised. "Oh no, Dr. Kong. I have a very different allegiance!"

Just then the train whistle blew, and people began to shove on board. "Dr. Kong, you have been a wonderful doctor, and a wonderful friend. I appreciate your help today."

"I hope that we can meet again, Li."

"And I as well," he replied. That familiar smile came across his face. He lifted his sack to his shoulder and stepped aboard. I waved until he was out of sight. I knew that I'd really miss him.

Several weeks later, amid the falling yellow leaves of autumn, I cycled past hundreds of people sweeping the street. They walked in lines down the street, each armed with a simple tree branch as a broom, piling the leaves into carts stationed along the way. At the front of their battalion marched a man beating a bass drum. Another clashed cymbals together and two more held a banner high. It read "Protect your health, keep Shanghai clean." As they paraded along, people from the sidewalk spontaneously took rakes or brooms and joined the cleanup procession, which grew as it went along.

This is really great, I thought. *These people are volunteering their time for the good of the community! People in America are usually too "busy" for things like this. Dr. Cheng did say that this was the goal of Marxism. But he did not say what motivates them to act better toward each other. I wonder what it is?*

On arrival at the hospital I left the bike parked in the courtyard and went to my new department, gastroenterology, where I'd be working for the winter. As a professor greeted me warmly, Dr. Cheng came by. He quickly led me into a back office. Pushing me inside, he poked his head outside the door, looked both ways, then silently closed the door. In the dim, stuffy room his countenance suddenly became quite serious. He looked more callous than usual. He scrutinized my face, looking down at me through squinting eyes. When he finally spoke, his words cut at me like an accusation.

"I know about you."

I looked at him helplessly. *Now even he is suspicious of me!* I thought. *Does he think I'm a spy or a terrorist or something?*

"I have heard that you are a Christian." He paused again, keeping the same expression. "Is this true?"

"Yes, it is," I replied with conviction.

"I was once a Christian." He sounded a little disappointed. Then he perked up. "But not anymore. Nevertheless, I'm very glad you're here. You've been a good influence."

I breathed a sigh of relief. "Thank you," I said.

Meeting adjourned, I found Dr. Tao and we entered a long ward lined with twelve beds on either side, each occupied by curious patients who were clearly sizing me up. In the center of the ward stood some potted flowers, and around a bare wooden table some men sat playing checkers.

"In this department you will deal with many diseases similar to those in America," Dr. Tao explained. "People with stomach ulcers are common here, as are those with liver cirrhosis. But there are some notable exceptions to what you are used to seeing. In our country, schistosomiasis, a small parasite from water snails, is the leading cause of liver cirrhosis, not alcohol, as it is in your country."

"I have heard that once this parasite gets into your system it never leaves," I said.

"Yes. It is a terrible health problem here." He continued, "You will also need to remember that gall bladder pain is not always due to stones, but may be caused by another intestinal parasite, a worm, if you will. They can crawl into the gall bladder and block it up. These parasites still pose a tremendous problem in the rural areas where sewage disposal is not good."

We continued to walk slowly along past each bed. "Another remarkable difference from America is that cancer of the stomach is much more common in the Orient than in your country. We don't know the reason exactly why this is so, but it probably has something to do with our diet."

We then came to a brief stop in front of a bed. "I'd like to assign your first patient, who arrived here this morning. Please take good care of him. I've seen him act in one of the Beijing operas here several times in the past."

He introduced me to the man, an obvious celebrity with graceful hand gestures and a penetrating voice. After a firm handshake, he presented me with the basin of blood he had vomited the night before. I pulled up a chair and talked with him a while. He said that his appetite had been poor, yet his abdomen had slowly increased in size. This did not seem to trouble him, however. He said, "I thought that all opera singers were supposed to be a little fat. I was just becoming like the others. But last night after the performance I began to vomit blood."

On examination I found excess fluid in his abdomen and an enlarged spleen. His blood test showed that he had also lost a lot of blood. It was likely that liver cirrhosis, as Dr. Tao had mentioned, was the cause of his illness. I reached for his chart and began to write down orders for his immediate care, which included a blood transfusion.

"Oh, that will hardly be possible," said Dr. Tao, looking over my shoulder as I wrote.

"Why is that?"

"There is very little blood donated here. Our blood bank is almost empty. We can only get blood for specific people in a prearranged fashion."

"But how can you have a hospital without blood?"

"Chinese are particularly infatuated with their personal health. Most feel that giving blood will hurt them. The philosophy goes something like this, 'If I have ten pints of blood in my body, then I must need ten pints to stay healthy and can't spare one to give up.'"

This was a puzzling situation. If the man should bleed any more, he might well die without the transfusion. Then I had an idea. What about his family? Families are usually strong in China, so they should be willing to help. It was at least worth a try.

I walked to the corridor outside the ward and called for the patient's family. A man stood up immediately. He introduced himself as the singer's uncle. I explained to him how critical the situation was.

"Oh, doctor, that sounds dreadful," said the middle-aged

fellow. He held a cane in one hand, a cigarette in the other. "Is there anything that you can do to save him?"

"Well, not much," I said in a purposely helpless manner. "But there is something that *you* can do."

His eyes lit up. "What can I do to help? I'll do anything!"

"Then you must find several people to donate blood for him," I said. "It is his only hope!"

The man was taken aback. "But isn't there any other way to help him? What about more traditional medicines?"

"No, none of that will do. Look, if he should die, you will probably have to take care of his family yourself!"

He suddenly changed his air. "Well . . . I would not want that to happen. I mean, I would not want him to die. He can have all of my blood. Won't that be enough?" he pleaded.

Now it was my turn to be taken aback. I was impressed at the success of this tactical maneuver. "I appreciate your willingness, but taking all of your blood wouldn't do you much good. Why don't you find some of his friends to help also?"

"Yes, I will do that," he said, looking more noble than before.

He turned and walked toward the stairway. I called after him, "I'll meet you in the laboratory at eleven o'clock."

When I returned to the ward, Dr. Tao met me. "How did it go?" he asked.

"Piece of cake!" I replied in English.

"Piece of cake?" he repeated and looked at me with a puzzled expression.

I could not help but say, "Oh, I am sorry, Dr. Tao. I forgot you don't understand jive."

He chuckled, remembering our earlier conflict with language. I put my arm around his shoulders and we walked out of the ward with big grins on our faces.

At the appointed time, Dr. Tao and I headed for the laboratory to check on the blood transfusion. The uncle was already there with three other adults. They were sitting in chairs, blood running from their veins into plastic containers.

"None of them seemed to mind being stuck with a needle," I commented.

"They are used to it. Contrary to their feelings about donating blood, most Chinese think that needles will help their health," replied Dr. Tao.

I gave him a puzzled look.

"Because of acupuncture!" he said.

While the man was receiving his transfusion, I took a break in our nearby office. There were a few other doctors there also, reading newspapers and relaxing. A thermos of hot water, perpetually filled from the kitchen, stood on the table. I sprinkled some tea leaves into the mug that Li Ming had given me and poured in the boiling water. I wondered how Li was doing. Given his condition, he could relapse into heart failure at any time.

One of the doctors noticed my guitar case on the floor, which I often carried to work to play in quiet moments.

"Dr. Kong, sing us a song!" commanded a friend.

"What would you like to hear?" I always enjoyed an audience.

"Oh, some folk songs, like you would sing at home."

I took out the instrument and perched it on my left knee. Several doctors were watching me now. "Have you ever heard of 'Oh Suzanna?' She is quite famous in America." They gave me a bewildered look, so I went ahead and began to sing in English, "Well, I come from Alabama with my banjo on my knee, and I'm bound . . ."

As I played on, heads started to poke around the door. Then, one by one, several of the nurses and students tiptoed inside to listen. A janitor sweeping on the balcony put his head through the open window. Even Dr. Cheng, who happened by, paused at the doorway.

After a round of applause one young man asked in broken English, "How could the sun be so hot that a person would freeze?" I told him that the weather in America can change very quickly.

Another spoke up. "Dr. Kong, please sing us an opera song."

"All right," I replied, "this is 'Caro Mio Ben.' It's an Italian art song. I learned it in high school."

After I started to sing the melody, the oddest thing happened. Another person seemed to be singing along with me. *Couldn't be*, I thought. *No one here would know this song.*

But it was true. The voice grew louder. I put down the guitar to investigate. I kept singing and walked out to the ward to find the opera singer sitting up in bed, blood running into his arm, harmonizing to 'Caro Mio Ben' with me at the top of his lungs. I walked quickly to his bed, and together we finished out the last refrain for the small crowd who had gathered to listen. They applauded wildly.

"Oh Dr. Kong," said Fei Chow, a woman doctor, "that was lovely!"

I bowed and smiled, thinking that perhaps singing was better for international friendship than sports!

When I arrived for the afternoon clinic, I found Dr. Tao had arrived before me and was examining a pathetic-looking figure. The son who had brought him in said that his father's name was Wo Wei. I was surprised when he said that his father was only fifty-six. He looked much older to me. His gray hair was falling out, and he had swollen eyes and hollow cheeks.

In trembling, slow words, he spoke to us. "I don't know what is wrong with me. I feel so tired, I can hardly move. I'm not even hungry. It started several years ago, but got better after my doctor gave me some steroid medicine to take. But you probably know our culture," he said, looking deliberately at me. "We don't like to swallow pills. So I stopped after a few months. The thing that bothers me most now is this terrible diarrhea, ten or twenty times a day."

The son explained that his father was a public servant who worked for the Communist Party, and who needed to return to his work as soon as possible.

We immediately admitted him to the hospital and per-formed some X-rays during the following week. These helped to confirm my suspicion that Wo Wei had ulcerative colitis, a disease of the large intestine. The medication that we gave him over the next several days began to help. But still, Wo Wei was very depressed because of the diarrhea. It caused him more often than not to be on the toilet, the one with the fading letters "WC" painted above it by some thoughtful Briton a century before. Part of the problem was toilet paper. The soft kind that is known in America was a privilege to the few who had money to spare. Wo, as everyone else, used the common, inexpensive kind. It was like sandpaper and contrib-uted to his misery.

A small breakthrough came one day when I noticed a medical student walk to Wo Wei's bedside. He pulled a roll of soft, fluffy pink toilet paper from his coat and gave it to the man. For the first time in a week Wo Wei grinned happily.

Later that morning I was surprised to find Dr. Cheng on his knees in the ward with several others, sweeping the floor. Others were carrying the bamboo poles from the hall to outside. When I asked what all the fuss was about I was told that we were to be visited by a noted San Francisco professor of gastroenterology. I hoped this might be a chance to enlist some expert help in Wo Wei's care.

After an hour the professor arrived at the ward with his translator and was introduced to the sea of Chinese physicians who gathered to meet him. As we went around the circle giving our names, he shot a glance in my direction, then a second, and then he said, "Well, I'll be. What in the world are you doing here?"

I told him the brief version of how I came to spend my first year of hospital residency in Shanghai.

He regained his composure after a moment and then said, "I can't believe you're actually doing this. Don't you think it's dangerous living here?" He must have forgotten that some of the English-speaking Chinese in the group might be offended by this question.

"Not at all. Really, there is almost no crime here," I replied. "I have felt more safe on the dark streets of Shanghai than I ever did in San Francisco in broad daylight."

"No, no. I mean, aren't you afraid that they might try to convince you to become a Communist?" He truly sounded concerned.

"They have not really tried. But there are actually some good things about what they are doing."

"This is amazing," he replied. "And do they pay you a salary?"

"Not as such, but I and the others get what we call 'food money.'"

The professor looked intrigued. "What is that?"

"It is an incentive plan, and rather capitalistic at that. The principle is that for every patient we see or operation we perform, we need extra calories for the energy to do the job.

The bigger the job, the more calories needed. For example, whenever I do an appendectomy, I receive a ticket for five cookies in the cafeteria. A stomach operation is good for ten cookies."

He chuckled. "That's quite a pragmatic plan! Still, be careful of these Chinese! Don't let them get into your mind."

"Thank you, doctor. I will remember that," I said politely. "Now, I have a question for you. There is a man whom I am caring for, with ulcerative colitis. Could I ask your opinion about his care?"

"Certainly! Lead the way."

I introduced him to Wo Wei, who seemed pleased to receive so much attention. The group formed a semicircle around him, and I explained the findings to our guest. He then examined Wo and asked me what kind of medications we were giving him. I gave him the list and as he read it, he gave me another surprised look.

"This drug is experimental in America. I only first heard of it a few months ago."

One of the doctors spoke up, "Oh, professor, we have been using it for years. It is very effective."

"You're really up to date," he replied. He then looked back at Wo Wei and asked, "Why is there a toothbrush taped to his thumb?"

His nurse turned red. "It's to keep his thumb from moving so that the IV line won't come out," she said bashfully. "I could not find anything else to use." I quickly translated her response.

Wo must have sensed that she had been put on the spot, for he added, "It's also very convenient for me. When I want to clean my teeth, I have the brush right here. Don't you think that it is a good idea?"

The professor was now very diplomatic. He explained that

this was not generally the practice in American hospitals. He smiled and promised to look into this innovation when he got home.

Later in the day the professor went back to the downtown hotel where he was staying, and I returned to the ward. Wo Wei waved for my attention and asked me the meaning of the professor's strange words. After I translated the morning's events he was encouraged a little. Still, it was clear that his recovery would be slow.

"How do you feel about being in the hospital for two long weeks?" I asked.

"Honestly, it is a much-needed rest for me. It has been years since I had a vacation. Being here has given me time to think about my work. Before coming to the hospital I was rewriting some of the political study books used in our primary schools. They are part of our curriculum. We believe that the greatest potential for China is in our youth, so it is essential to train them in the principles of Marxism from an early age."

I perceived that I was on the brink of discovering just how they were trying to improve individual behavior, as Dr. Cheng had foretold. I also remembered Pao Chu in Hong Kong. He would have wanted to be in on this conversation. I was all ears.

He continued. "You see, Dr. Kong, by having the state control all production and employment we can eliminate the unfair social classes and the exploitation of workers that is seen in your country. Everyone in China, be he a peasant or a professor, receives a similar wage and type of housing. The surgeons in your hospital are paid not much more than those street sweepers outside."

"So what is the overall goal of the Marxists?" I asked.

"We are working for the common good of our society. We

want to develop a people who won't be selfish in wanting possessions or power, but will rather work hard, motivated by the knowledge that they are helping each other. You see, Marxism is far more than an economic system. It is a philosophy, a way of looking at life. We want to create the New Man."

Here I stopped him. "The New Man?"

"Yes. There is no way that a perfect society can exist without a fundamental change in human nature. People need to be liberated from their selfishness. What we leaders must do is to transform people from being egotistical, aggressive, greedy, and immoral into becoming new social beings. The New Man is, or will be, one who is cooperative, loving, neighborly, and eager to share. Many have tried to create the New Man in the past, but have failed. They have used religion, knowledge, technology, and genetics. But we are not like them. We will not fail! We have the most enlightened plan!"

"This is a very admirable purpose you have, Wo," I said. "I have thought about the same things myself. How do you intend to change people? What is your plan?"

"We are doing this by educating the public in Marxist principles, by reprogramming their values and concepts. Once everyone believes and practices these things we won't even need a government to control them. We will have a perfect state! The people will take care of themselves, but without succeeding in this reeducation of the people, we will never attain true Communism."

"Your government is very strong. Some even call it oppressive."

"This is necessary for now. We need a strong party to lead the country and oppose anyone who resists this transformation and our ultimate goal. We also have to have strong laws to force people to be equal until the society is filled with New Men. After that, the laws and education won't be necessary. I am part of this, Dr. Kong. It is my life. And what about you? You seem to be interested in this kind of revolution as well."

"Yes, I am. I have been impressed that your country has the courage to address such issues on a national level. I'd like to find out more about what you believe."

"I'd be happy to teach you. You should consider becoming one of us. We need people motivated like you!"

Wo Wei shifted under his blankets in the cool room and cracked some dried sunflower seeds, swallowing a handful before continuing. "Still, there are some problems in this reeducation process." His demeanor became more serious. "Take my two sons, for example. They both still live at home with me, but my wife left us years ago. They work in a steel mill, providing valuable material to help build our country. They contribute much, but when they come home from a long day they often complain and ask me things like, 'Why should we work so hard if we're all going to get paid the same amount anyway?' or 'Whenever I see someone working hard at the mill it makes me look bad and I despise him.' Both are also very concerned about owning a TV and having new bicycles."

"All of this seems to be contrary to what you believe," I said. "It seems to go against the entire idea of Marxism. What do you think is wrong with them?"

"I don't know exactly," replied Wo. "They have attended classes in Marxist ideals all through school, and, of course, I have taught them the principles of class struggle and equality ever since they were children. Even now at the steel mill these weekly indoctrination classes continue. The teaching process must not be quite effective. This is why I'm rewriting the books that are used.

"Our relationship with Russia is not good now, but they helped us to establish our country along Marxist lines. One of their thinkers was Ilyichov. He said, 'The Party considers the education of the New Man to be the most difficult task in the Communist transformation of society. . . . Unless we uproot the moral principles of the bourgeois world and educate people in the spirit of Communist morality and a spiritually regenerated man, it is not possible to build a Communist society.' He was so right. Unless we can change people, we will fail."

A nurse approached us to take Wo for an X-ray. As he departed, Wo called, "Come back again and we can talk some more!"

I left the ward, thinking about our conversation. *Certainly people are influenced strongly by the ideas they have. What they are trying to do makes sense. In fact, I remember hearing it said that China may well have the most powerful propaganda campaign of all time—but at least they are trying to change the nature of people, rather than just picking up the pieces.*

The shadows were already quite long as I walked out of the tree-lined emergency entrance. Here stood several hundred people, as they did each evening, waiting in line to go inside to visit patients. If they all went inside at once, sheer chaos would result from the crowds, so the director, Dr. Cheng, had devised a system. One hundred passes were available and given to the first hundred visitors who arrived. Everyone else entered in turn with a pass obtained from each visitor exiting the building.

Suddenly there was a familiar voice behind me.

"Dr. Kong!"

I turned. It was Li Ming! He had gained some weight and glowed with delight. "It's so good to see you again, Dr. Kong!"

"And you as well, Li." We shook hands warmly. "I'm surprised to see you back in Shanghai. How is your family?"

"Oh, they are very well. In fact, they are here with me. Tomorrow is my checkup with Dr. Tao." He grew more excited. "Some friends in my hometown gathered the money so that we could all make the trip together. My daughter has never been to the city before. We are also going to stay in town for several weeks and help care for my invalid mother. But, Dr. Kong, the reason I came down tonight was just to invite you to have dinner with us. We're staying at my sister's home."

My only other option for dinner was to have noodles at a street cafe. I quickly accepted his offer, and we walked toward the bus stop together.

"You must have some very special friends in your hometown to help your entire family to come here," I commented. It seemed like the kind of spontaneous giving that Wo Wei talked about wanting.

"Yes, they are wonderful! There is a community of supportive and understanding people there."

"Is there a Marxist education program there?" I asked.

Li continued to smile. "No, not at all. What we have is different. My life was different before, but I began to spend time with several men in my town, and listen to them talk about—"

Just then the bus came to a screeching stop in front of us. The doors were flung open and the sea of workers standing with us on the curb washed us aboard. There were feet being stepped on, elbows flying, and tempers rising. The conductor closed the door on the mob. Then, as the bus jolted off, he called for tickets. Li and I each pulled out four cents and passed it to the conductor, who in turn handed us a tiny receipt. Next to us stood an elderly man dressed in a dark blue coat. He fumbled about in his pockets and looked frustrated.

Li Ming noticed him and spoke up, "How can I help you, sir?"

"I seem to have forgotten my money. I thought that it was right here! I'll just have to get off at the next stop." He looked down at his feet.

"I'll take care of it!" said Li. "It would be a pleasure." He reached into his pocket.

"Oh, you don't understand," the man said. "You see, I'm going to my parent's home. It's all the way to Ja Ding. The ticket costs eighty cents."

"That is half a day's wages!" I said. I knew that Li could not have very much money.

"Don't fear, I will help," said Li, ignoring my comment. He handed his coins to the conductor. The man breathed a sigh of relief and said to Li, "I do not know what to say, except that you are a model citizen!"

Our street was then announced and we stepped off the bus into a narrow, cobblestone alley that led us up to a small wooden door. After we knocked, a resident of the first floor opened it for us. We walked through a small courtyard lined with tomato plants and climbed a narrow, rickety staircase through the house. I noticed that Li puffed a little as we climbed the creaking stairs, dodging clothes hung in the passage to dry.

On a small landing stood two full-sized chickens. They were bound to each other by a string leading from the foot of one to the foot of the other. Li told me that they had been growing here for months in preparation for the New Year's holiday meals. Escape was impossible, he explained. Though they were not tied to any fixture, whenever one began to flee, the other would restrain him. They must have had similar intentions to escape, but neither could enlist the aid of the other. There seemed to be some profound meaning to this predicament.

His sister's home was situated on the top of the century-old tenant building and was more spacious than most I had visited. Li's delicate wife and small daughter met us at the door and led me into their bright quarters. His wife looked happier than when I had seen her last. A round table had been set with more than twenty kinds of food. There was a ceramic spoon and chopsticks at each place. While yet more dishes were being brought in, we seated ourselves on a sofa and munched on peanuts. Li talked about how the Chinese women's volleyball team had crushed the United States team in international competition. We chuckled, and I tried to change the subject by commenting on the furnishings of the room.

The ceiling was low, sloping slightly toward walls that were covered with warping wallpaper. Several traditional paintings adorned the walls, with a poem written in ancient letters on each. A bookcase was filled with novels and picture albums. Several ceramic dolls on the top held the brief attention of a playful white kitten that seemed to go unnoticed as it roamed about the room. The corners of the room were filled with three wooden beds consisting of a thin mat on top of a rope net strung between the frame. At the foot of the beds were neatly folded quilts, and pillows with pretty silk cases.

As I looked, my eyes fell on a very elderly woman on one of the beds. Li said that this was his mother, and led me over to meet her. She was too infirm to rise. After a bow of respect, I drew near as she whispered, "We are so happy and honored to have you as our guest. It has been fifty years since an American visited our home. We are grateful that you could come be with us." Because she used Shanghai dialect, Li translated, but her intent was perfectly clear.

As we took our places at the table, Li asked, "Dr. Kong, do you know the proverb of the fish?"

I returned his question with a puzzled look. "No, I have not heard that one yet."

He spoke slowly and deliberately and with a big smile. "If you eat the tail of a fish, then you can swim!" He laughed so hard that I could not help but join him. I thought, *If laughter is the best medicine, no wonder he recovered.*

In typical Eastern dining custom, each person reached across the table to take a food from the serving dishes and place it on the dish of another. Then, in turn, the other would load up the plate of his companion. Boiled shrimp, fried mushrooms, bean curd, and duck eggs were soon followed by river crabs, diced eel, sliced pig stomach, and dumplings. It was nearly all good, but the pig stomach I could have done without. Next came the sweet pork, fried pig tendons, and a soup of snake meat and shark fins. This soup, I had heard, was an ancient recipe of the emperors. It was also a strong tonic known to increase one's sexual prowess!

A choice of rice wine or beer washed the meal down, and the feast was finished with a large bowl of rice for each participant, to ensure that no one should go away hungry. Following the meal, I was approached by Li's shy four-year-old, her long pigtails swinging over a pretty cotton jumper. She challenged me to a round of animal checkers.

The game was new to me and consisted of a checkerboard with some lakes painted on it. Each of us had a group of animals symbolized by various checker pieces. They were lined up on either side of the board. The object was to move all of one's animals from one side of the board to the other without being killed or eaten by the opponent.

In the opening moves she used her tiger to turn away my attacking rabbit. In retaliation, I moved a cat to pounce on her bird. To the delight of the onlooking family, she avoided my capture of her bird by bringing a lion from the rear. He ate my offending cat!

I discovered that I was losing. As a last resort, I moved my elephant forward. It charged past her tiger and bear. My elephant appeared victorious until without warning, her mouse set the elephant in terror. With no escape possible, my poor elephant was driven into a lake, where he drowned. She quickly moved all of her animals to my side and announced her victory. Laughing uproariously, everyone clapped and congratulated her on beating Dr. Kong.

It was good to be with Li again. As I rode home on the bus, I wondered again what made him so cheerful and gracious. I resolved to find out as soon as I had the chance.

Pop the Bubble

*T*HE CHILLY DAYS OF AUTUMN arrived. The days grew shorter and it turned bitterly cold. It was obvious from my daily bike trip to work that winter brought with it a different pace of life. Everyone now wore huge blue overcoats instead of light jackets. Underneath, they also wore several layers of shirts, perhaps their entire wardrobe. Their trousers bulged from long underwear. Though the winds were freezing, few people wore a cap. Only a small set of muffs protected their ears. I noticed that the bird owners had left the parks. Still, the old men preferred their checker games outside, warmth furnished by thick clothing and warm company. Only the most dedicated people continued to come for morning exercises, however. These people were often older and well-disciplined in appearance. Each morning they would follow the self-appointed exercise leader in a series of slow, graceful motions. At one moment they would sweep their hands as if to fly, and at the next, crouch as if preparing to jump. They exercised for beauty, not for sweat.

Just to the north of Shanghai one could see the great Yenze River. One government policy for energy conservation was that no homes south of the Yenze would receive fuel for heating. Lack of coal kept most homes so cold that ice collected in the wash pans. Washed clothes froze dry on the lines outside, and frozen ducks hung from windowsills, where they would be kept until a holiday. I never encountered a person with frostbite, though, for they had learned to care for themselves. They seemed to accept these hardships as a way of life.

It was more difficult for me. I slept fully clothed and under several blankets. Occasionally my shaving cream froze in its container, and the water froze in the pipes, but the greatest challenge was showering. Once a week I forced myself into the chilly water for a much-needed scrub.

At the hospital, physician and patient alike were dressed as if for an Arctic exploration. We waddled about like penguins in our stuffy outfits. Each morning my patients unbuttoned, unzipped, and unsnapped ten to fifteen layers for examination by my cold hands. They could not help but jump when I touched them. However, Wo Wei always greeted me with a warm handshake. His secret was a jar of hot water concealed beneath the blankets. We talked together one bitterly cold morning as we both sat shivering.

"Why do the people here put up with the fact that there is no fuel for heat?" I asked.

"Well, to start with, it is for the good of the country. For another, there is little choice. We are not able to provide heat to everyone. The demand is too great."

"Do workers ever stage a strike to press their demands?"

"Oh, no. Nothing like that. We can not allow any strikes or unions or any such thing. This would undermine the progress of the country."

My eyes caught sight of a steam heat radiator in the corner of the ward. Wo Wei explained that it had probably been disconnected from the wall when the British left years before, for there was no coal for the boiler. The large buildings downtown had been treated in the same way.

"We don't have the resources for luxuries like heat," said

Wo, "but perhaps we will someday. There is a proverb that explains this situation. There once was a man in ancient China who bought a precious sword. He wore it hanging at his side. He was the envy of all his neighbors.

"One day, he set out across a river in an open boat with a friend at the oars. As he leaned out over the edge to look at his appearance in the water, his precious sword suddenly fell in with a splash. Remarkably, the man remained calm and collected. Pulling a knife from his pocket, he slowly made a mark on the side of the boat. Then he rested back against the stern.

"While continuing to row, his friend questioned him. 'Your precious sword fell into the river! Why didn't you immediately jump in to retrieve it? And what good will marking the boat do you?'

"The man replied, 'This mark indicates the place where my sword dropped in. When we reach the other side and tie up to the dock it will be convenient for me to jump into the water just at this point that I have marked, and pull out my sword.'"

I often had trouble understanding parables, and this time was no different. Wo must have noticed, for he continued.

"You see, this man missed the fact that life goes on and circumstances continue to change. Rather than recognize that they had moved from the spot of the accident, he thought nothing had changed. But life does change, and we must be able and ready to adjust to whatever challenges it presents to our country."

I suddenly remembered that it was Christmas Day and that I was to meet with Keith and the other Americans that evening. I wondered what Wo thought of Christianity.

"Wo Wei," I said, "I am a Christian and today is an important holiday for us. I wonder what you . . ."

He immediately cut me off. "Now stop that! There is no

power in religion, but deception. All that it does is pacify the people. It has no benefit at all." He looked a little perturbed that I mentioned the subject at all.

I was surprised that he was offended. He usually seemed like such an open-minded person. "Why are you so against faith in God?" I asked.

"What we need is loyalty," he replied, "loyalty to the Party above all. I can not tolerate any ideas contrary to Marxism. It will dilute the efforts that we are trying to make."

"I am truly impressed with the intentions that you and the Party have. But, just to be fair, have you ever considered the message of Jesus?"

Wo pulled the blankets up over himself and lay back in his bed. He did not answer me. I did not feel that I had hurt Wo's feelings, only expanded his mind. But he did appear tired from the conversation.

A nurse walked up and asked me to see an anemic man who had just been admitted. He was from Hunan Province. Wo waved a good-bye as I followed her to a nearby ward and entered through its curved archway.

It was not difficult to determine which person this patient might be. Seated upright on a cot next to a bare concrete wall was a very pale man. His wizened face held a long, narrow beard and the wrinkles on his forehead seemed like deep ridges. In one hand he held a sketch book, in the other he clutched a cane.

I asked him what the problem was. In a dignified yet humble manner he described how for years he had suffered from a blood disease. Fatigue and dizziness had sent him on numerous occasions to local clinics where iron and vitamins were given to him in an effort to correct his marked anemia, but without success. I was impressed by the presence of this man and could not help but ask his occupation.

"I am an artist and a poet, a historian and a philosopher," he replied. "A thinker of this generation."

I was not surprised at all. It fit his character. After examining him, I took a drop of his blood to the laboratory and put it on a glass slide. I stained the blood cells and placed the slide on a microscope. The instrument did not have an electric light, so I adjusted a glass reflector towards the sun coming through a window. The shape of the blood cells was normal, but they were larger than usual, and a great many more were present than I had expected.

Armed with this data, I returned to talk with the artist. I explained my suspicions to him and was careful to avoid the word *cancer* for the moment. I recommended that we perform a bone marrow examination to get a better look at his blood.

"Is this like acupuncture?" he asked in a gentle tone. "I would not mind that at all."

"Well, in a way," I explained, "only the needle is larger." After a few questions about the pain involved, he consented.

In the afternoon I returned to see him. First I washed the skin over his hip and injected an anesthetic into his skin with a special needle. Then I bored a hole into the hipbone and drew out some of the bone marrow. After the needle was removed, a dressing was placed on his skin. He winced only once, but it was enough to make me ask myself why we so often have to hurt people in order to help them. He then was taken to a bed. A few days would be required to study the bone marrow in the laboratory.

I left the hospital earlier than usual that day and started off for the Shanghai Teachers' College. While I rode, I wondered what my family was doing that day. Letters took two weeks to get home, and a phone call was quite expensive. I really missed my parents, but I compensated for this by making friends wherever I could. And I was looking forward to spending Christmas with my American friends.

When I arrived, I found Keith waiting at the gate.

"Hello, Dr. Kong!" he called out. "I am happy that you could come!"

"I'm glad to make it. I suppose by the time I leave China I'll have been everywhere in Shanghai on a bike." I got off and parked it. "Tonight, please call me Nicholas. I've had enough of doctoring for the day."

"I don't suppose you ever celebrated Christmas in China before, have you?"

"No, I sure haven't!"

When we got inside, I found the others assembled around a large, round table. Holiday cheer filled the room. I was introduced again to Michael, Tina, Kathy, and Kirt. They were all from the east coast. We sat down to a catered meal from the college cafeteria, and afterwards someone called for Christmas carols. With a chopstick as a conducting baton, I took my place as the choir director. We sang several songs and exchanged some potluck gifts. Afterward, Keith and I sat on the balcony and talked.

"What do you think about this country?" he asked me.

"What do you mean?"

"I'm referring to the political oppression. Doesn't it get to you? I often feel smothered by it all."

"So do I at times," I replied. "But it's not all bad. The leaders seem to have good intentions."

Keith looked surprised. "Do you mean you support them? Are you a Marxist?"

"Of course not. But I *am* for China. I want the best for this country," I said earnestly. "America has its drawbacks, too. The Chinese are really trying to address their problems.

"One question I had when I came to China was 'How can

you make people behave better toward one another?' The Chinese have found one way." I suddenly realized it as I spoke. "One way is by educating the people in healthy values."

"I don't think that it is worth sacrificing my personal freedom for society," said Keith. "There is only so much that one can do to help other people."

"You are giving up too easily, Keith."

"Well, maybe I am, but I'm not going to listen to any of the ideas the Chinese have."

Our conversation was becoming tense. After a moment, Tina came out and offered us some of the cookies she had made. I changed the subject to volleyball. I knew that was safe.

I took the trolley home later that evening and got off at the Shanghai Second Medical College. The guard at the entrance swung open the large gate for me. Immediately ahead was a political slogan on a wall. It reminded everyone to hold high the banner of Marxism. As I walked along, I remembered what I had been told about the place. The campus, with its large lecture halls, laboratories, sports field, and dormitories, had been established as Aurora University around 1910. The designers, financiers, and instructors were French, and many were Catholic priests. Very few people here still remembered the days when the campus was a place for lively exchange between the culture and knowledge of both East and West. Now the only foreigners in the college were some Africans and myself.

These blacks represented several developing nations. They had come to China to study textiles, railroading, or medicine as part of a cooperative program to help their countries. These students were severely looked down upon by the Chinese people, just as I had seen at the basketball game. They were kept isolated from the Chinese students in dormitories of their own, and often they were not allowed to attend classes with other Chinese students. On the streets many merchants shunned them. They said that they detested the music and dancing of the Africans. A month before, the blacks had held a boycott of the school cafeteria. They did not come to any of the meals that were prepared. This was to draw attention to their ill treatment from a professor who had called one of them an animal. All that the boycott seemed to do, however, was to make matters worse. "So much for racial equality in China," I thought.

I passed the sleepy watchman at the door of my dorm and saw a few students watching an old movie on TV. After climbing five flights of stairs, I unlocked the door of my simple home. It was one room of painted concrete walls. There was a swing-out window at one end, overlooking a courtyard where I hung my laundry to dry. A shelf held a few essential books, including the Surgery Textbook by Dumphy and Way, and a Beijing travel guide. A copy of *Gulliver's Travels* provided entertainment for my leisure moments. A small desk, a hard bed covered with a worn straw mat, and a couple of scroll paintings completed the decor. I took off my clothes and washed them out by hand, a nightly task. Then I laid out my running shoes for the morning track meet.

I had been working out in the mornings for several weeks in preparation for the Shanghai Invitational Track Meet. The authorities of the Second Medical College had asked me to represent them. In the process I had made several friends with whom I ran regularly. It seemed that working out together was better for international friendship than competing.

At 6 A.M. sharp, exactly as they did every day, military march tunes blared across campus. This woke all but the deaf.

Following the music, the national news was reported in crisp Mandarin. I rolled out into the freezing air and pulled on some sweatpants and a warm shirt. I had to move fast to keep warm. As I shaved, the soap froze to my face. Worse yet, no razor blades had come in the care package I'd just received. I had been using the same razor for a month.

Downstairs in the kitchen I found that the cooks had laid wagers on who would win the various races. Several students were already in place at the bare wooden tables when I arrived. A few Cambodian girls in their brightly colored robes sat laughing in one corner. When I took a seat, the familiar cook with a perpetual, though toothless, smile brought out a fried egg sandwich and a glass of hot milk for me. The milk was saturated with sugar, but it certainly made me feel warm inside. As I left, the cook flashed me the thumbs up sign wishing me success.

Several busloads of athletes had already arrived at the track when I got there. Banners had been strung across the road announcing the event, and soon thousands of spectators arrived. Each player wore the sporting uniform of his school, and march tunes sounded from speakers overhead. Several athletes were doing stretches on the ground. I thought of my running days in high school. Neither my coaches then, nor I myself, would ever have thought that I'd be running in a place like this!

The morning's competition included the high jump, the shot put, and the discus throw. Then came the javelin throw and relay races. Amid the cheering of onlookers, a well-known soccer coach of the medical school approached me, a lab report in hand. I thought, *Boy, they track me down everywhere!*

"Dr. Kong, I know it's your day off, but I just want to ask you something. I had this liver function blood test done last week. They told me not to eat anything for the test, and I haven't eaten since then. It has been four days now! I thought that if I did eat, something might damage my liver. I am so hungry now!"

I looked at the paper and the numbers. They were all normal. I assured him of this and he breathed a sigh of relief. He immediately walked off toward a noodle restaurant on the corner.

As the sun climbed higher, the first call came for the 400 meter race, filling me with intense feelings of nostalgia as I thought of my high-school running years. However, I also remembered the pain of my previous races. After I finished stretching and jogging in place to warm up, I hurried to the starting line. Dr. Cheng stopped me on the way and reminded me that the honor of the school was at stake.

Elimination heats were run first. The competition was not difficult and I tried to conserve my energy as much as possible for the final race. Six contenders for the finals remained, representing several Shanghai colleges. As we lined up at the starting line, I shook hands with one of the other runners. In turn, he offered to run ahead of me to hand me a towel at the finish line! The starting judge placed me in the outside lane, the worst possible position, for you can't see the other runners behind you.

He then began calling the starting sequence in Shanghai dialect. As I turned to ask him to speak Mandarin, he fired the gun. Question answered! We sprinted down the track. I could see the spectators pressing close. At my left in lane five, I heard pounding feet and a short man shot ahead of the pack, but after the first turn petered out. In lane two, dirt flying from his cleats, came a student from the First Medical College, our rival school. He appeared invincible with his strong thighs and pumping arms. As we came into the second turn, however, the tall man in lane four bolted into the lead. I knew that he and I would be neck-and-neck to the end.

Excited by the fierce competition, the crowd screamed, "Ja yo, Ja yo!" ("Add oil! Go faster!").

In the final stretch and a meter behind, I forced my legs forward, doubting if I could close the gap. The pain in my legs was stabbing and I thought I'd fall. At the finish line, however, the leader stumbled. We collapsed into the arms of the spectators.

I was lying on the ground. I could not move, though I could hear the applause. Pain shot through my entire body and I vomited. Then I heard the announcer say that the race was an even draw! The fans cheered and someone lifted me to my feet. My head spun. A fellow physician came up and quickly examined me.

"You are suffering from a severe ice cream deficiency!" he said. A host of friends promptly carried me to the refreshment booth and we corrected the problem.

After the meet was over, I went back to my room and washed up. It was easier now that the air was warmer from the afternoon sun. I did not have any plans for that night and decided to take a walk on the famous Nan Jing Road. This led down to the Huangpu River, which winds through Shanghai. There was little other entertainment available, other than the over-crowded movie theaters or an occasional concert or play. Some others on the street had the same idea as I. Several groups of young people walked by; usually someone held a radio. I was soon joined by a few men who were eager for conversation. I was thankful for my Chinese dress and the growing shadows that kept me from drawing too large a crowd.

The four of us strode abreast past the locked shops and office buildings. A few traffic lights and automobiles lighted the street as sleet began to pour down. I was curious about what jobs my companions held. One explained that all three of them were workers at a steel factory. He said that he fed coal into a furnace, while another handled the molten cherry-red metal with a crane. The third, a little older than the others, was a foreman at a loading dock.

"How did you get these jobs?" I asked.

"After I finished high school," said one, "all I could do was go down to the government employment office and see if they could assign me somewhere. My brother has a little bicycle repair shop, but he didn't need me. So I just waited on a list for about eight months, like my friends, and then I was assigned a place at the factory. It is a very dirty place and unbearably hot in the summertime. There are also a lot of accidents from the heavy equipment."

"If you don't like it, can you change your job?" I asked.

"It's pretty difficult," he replied. "Only a few are able to do it. I have tried before because my wages are so low. I'd really like to get married, but can't with the money I'm getting now."

Another spoke up. "I have the same sort of problem. I am thirty-one and still living at home so that I can share expenses with my parents. Of course, they want me to stay around, and Shanghai is so crowded that there is hardly any place to move to. Besides, you have to be married to get a house of your own."

"Why is that?"

"All the houses are assigned to us. You just can't move anywhere you want. It is all controlled. When I get married, my wife and I will go apply for a place of our own. But if it does not come through, we'll have to put off our marriage or live with one of our parents. I don't know which would be the worse!"

I challenged them: "We all know that these are big problems that everyone shares. But you are working for the good of your country! You should be proud of the sacrifices that you are making for one another."

They all looked at me with disbelief. "You mean that you actually believe that stuff?" said one.

"Sure. It is essential for all of us to put up with some difficulties if things are to be any better for the country," I replied.

"We gave up on listening to all that political education stuff a long time ago," he said. "It does not work! We just want to have fun and live a comfortable life." The others nodded.

I said to myself, *Well, Wo Wei has a long way to go!*

We arrived at the water's edge and stood for a moment beneath the trees, watching a string of barges being pulled slowly up river by a lone tug. The thumping sound of its diesel engine ricocheted from the hulls of neighboring ships, echoing toward us like cannon fire. One of the ships flew a Greek national flag from its stern. Greek merchants had probably penetrated every harbor of the world, and Shanghai was no exception. I called out a greeting in Greek toward the ship, and moments later the deck was lined with sailors. Doubtless they were discussing what Chinaman had learned to speak Greek!

Walking away from the shore, we heard music coming from a group of young people ahead. As we got closer, I saw their leader at the center, guitar in hand. He was singing clearly and the others followed along as they strolled down the street. The four of us slipped to the rear of the group to get a better look, but I was soon discovered when the leader stopped under a street lamp. The others crowded around closely. Several wore black vinyl coats with turned-up collars, and smoked cigarettes. The men wore tight jeans and thin leather belts. The women likewise were clad in tight slacks and wore their black hair down. Some even had on a little makeup. I borrowed the guitar and set it on my knee. Immediately there was a command performance at hand.

"One of the main reasons I came to China," I said in Mandarin, "was to see a live dragon." They laughed. "In my search, I went and talked to the eldest men in Shanghai. One said that years ago he had seen one early in the morning by a river. However, you should know that the dragon is not unique to the East as many people think. America also has its own dragon."

They looked at me with expressions of surprise. And so I began to softly sing, "Puff, the Magic Dragon." The tune came easily to the onlookers, who began to hum along. Some joined arms and swayed to the music. For a moment, whatever barriers there were between East and West melted away under that streetlight.

Afterward, I handed the guitar back to the leader and the crowd dispersed. My factory friends invited me to have a warm drink. We entered the first coffee shop on the road. This was actually an old restaurant, which catered to the street people in the evenings. Friends sat huddled together in the cold, talking and joking. Steaming hot tea was brought to us. It was saturated with coarsely ground sugar that had settled to the bottom. I warmed my numb fingers with the teacup.

Suddenly an elderly man announced that closing time had come. Without any hesitation, he rudely pulled chairs from under the guests and placed them upside down on the tables, in spite of the crashing glasses. Some women screamed, and most instantly headed for the door. Quickly, so as to avoid this abuse, we downed our hot drinks and went out into the cold night.

When we reached a trolley station, I said farewell to my

new friends and I jumped on the bus. It wasn't as congested at this time of night. Quickly I bought a three-cent ticket and found a place to stand. At my feet sat an aging woman with several chickens and ducks stuffed into a net at her feet. They squawked with every jolt. At her side an old gentleman with sparse whiskers sat nodding sleepily. A couple carried their baby, covered with heavy blankets.

I thought of my conversation with the young factory workers. In spite of all of their political education, none of the ideas seemed to have stuck. They seemed just as self-centered as anyone else I knew.

At station after station we stopped to exchange passengers. At one, a farmer with vegetables in two bags hung at either end of a pole called out for the conductor to wait for a moment. He tried to lift the pole, but could hardly budge the load. Panic set in as he realized that in seconds the door would close if he could not lift the load and get on board. I knew that he might wait an hour before another bus arrived. Unexpectedly, a young fellow appeared from the dark street, raised the bundles in one motion, and set them on the bus. The farmer clambered on board and the door slammed shut before the farmer could thank him.

I wonder whether that was Li Ming? I thought.

The following day, the hospital was alive with talk of the track meet. Dr. Cheng, in particular, came by and congratulated me on my victory for the school. I was happy that I had run. Now, more than ever, they seemed to accept me as a part of their team. It was a victory for us all. Dr. Tao also gave me hearty praise. Then his expression became more serious.

"Yesterday I examined the bone marrow of Zhange, the artist. He clearly is suffering from chronic leukemia. This is what caused him to be so anemic. I went to his room to tell him myself since he did not have any family here. The poor fellow just cried. I felt awkward and didn't know what to do to comfort him. The other patients felt uncomfortable as well and began to leave. We just sat together in silence."

"I'm sorry," I said. "It must have been hard to tell him."

"You know, we usually only tell the family if it is bad news like this, but then the most amazing thing happened—Li Ming came into the room. You remember that I had seen him in the clinic a few weeks ago when he came back from the countryside for a checkup. He sat down next to the artist and cried, too! He may still be there now."

I walked to Zhange's room and opened its heavy doors. There sat Li Ming, next to the sobbing man. They did not notice me enter, so I just stood there. They spoke quietly in the Shanghai dialect. The only part I understood was when the artist said, "This is the end of my life! All of my friends are miles away. Thank you for staying with me."

As I walked back to Dr. Tao's office, the words of a professor in medical school came back to me. "Only nice people get leukemia." So true, the world over.

Knocking on the door, I found that Dr. Tao was still in. I took a seat on a wooden stool and waited. Faded curtains covered a lone window. In a corner stood an old desk with a huge Chinese typewriter on it. The professor stood at a porcelain sink, washing his hands.

"We should begin treatment soon," I said.

"Yes, but let's rest for a moment," he replied. He seemed to want to talk.

"Where was it that you went to college?" I asked.

"I attended the Saint John's Medical School. This was built in Shanghai by the University of Pennsylvania in 1879. I was fortunate to attend it, for it was the first Western medical school in Chinese history. That is my diploma there. Many of the instructors were Americans and Britons."

"So you must speak English well!" I said, surprised.

"Yes, I can understand what you say when you talk in English, but it is hard for me to speak any more. It brings back bad memories." He moved to the old rugged desk and sat down.

"What memories?" I asked.

"I will tell you. My education was interrupted for several years by the Japanese invasion. After the war I went back to school again, but many things had changed. The Communist Party was now in power in Shanghai. They controlled the college and taught us that the only reason these Westerners had come here was to establish colonies and to exploit us. It is true that some, particularly the British and French, wanted to do just that, but I believe that my instructors had worked here out of compassion and a sincere desire to help us—not for money or nationalism."

Tao continued to looked tense, so I decided to fix us something to drink. I took some shriveled tea leaves from a bag on his desk and dropped them into two cups. After pouring in hot water from a thermos, I handed a cup to Dr. Tao. He held the cup absent-mindedly as he continued his story.

"Mao was a great leader, and he and the Party soon had control of all China. At first there was a lot of celebration. But then they started to take the land and the stores away from the people and to tell us where to live. Mao said that this was necessary in order to eliminate the class structure.

"We were all forced to attend meetings that were supposed to reeducate us into thinking like real Marxists. The political leader at the hospital said that as people became better, they would begin to take responsibility for society and for themselves. He said that eventually we wouldn't need any government at all. We would become a sort of New Man, who cares for other people and has a community consciousness. For example, if I wrote a letter and needed to send it to another village, my neighbor would take it there out of the goodness of his heart. We would not need a postal service."

"That sounds like a wonderful objective," I said, "but how can people really become so giving?"

"The key, Mao said, was reeducation. We needed to have meetings and classes to teach us the principles of Marxism. If this were done long enough, the theory goes, the people would change. And until that time, to ensure that change did take place, the Communist Party would run the country, until it was not needed any more."

He stopped a moment and looked out of the doorway, as if to see whether anyone else was around. He looked satisfied and turned to me again.

"The Communist Party made lots of promises to us after the war. They said that we would now be free and prosperous, that we were establishing some kind of heaven on earth. But actually, we were ruled with an iron hand. The Party took control of all the farms, factories, businesses, and hospitals in the country, in addition to my school. The Marxists said that the fields and factories belonged to all of us, but we could not object to anything they wanted to do. We were forced to study these Marxist ideals. We could not object in any way without the threat of being expelled. I have studied Communism before. It says nothing about restricting individual freedom of choice. The reason we were restricted was so that the Party could stay in power. China has always been ruled by some kind of emperor. The Party had become the new landlords," he said bitterly.

"You must have been terribly disappointed."

Dr. Tao paused a moment and took a drink of tea. "I was, but it was only the beginning. In 1966 began the ten years of our 'Cultural Revolution.' This was the worst yet. During this time, Chairman Mao tried to put down the intellectuals and other leaders in our country. Perhaps he thought that we were too smart and might try to oppose him. For several years they would not let me practice medicine. I had to show up for work, but I simply swept the halls and cleaned the bathrooms of the hospital. This was supposed to humble me and keep me from being too proud of my skills. They thought that I represented capitalism because I had attended an English-speaking college! Well, it did humble me, but every day I saw patients die at the hands of young paramedics and nurses who did not know what they were doing out there. When I tried to correct them, I was laughed at in return.

"The Communists insisted that we participate in political meetings. These were held almost every day, wherever there was a work unit. The Red Guards were the young people who ran the revolution. They were guarding Marxism, or so they thought. They ran the meetings also. If someone was not radically supporting Mao, he would be criticized in public. One of the men I once went to school with was accused of not being loyal because he was the son of a banker, though he had done nothing wrong. They put him in stocks and later burned his home.

"This same type of persecution was directed against professors, engineers, students, and technicians all over China. Anyone who was previously in authority and not radically supportive of Mao was ostracized. Of course, the country was in chaos, but there was nothing we could do to stop it. There were great rallies held, even here in the hospital, in which people would stand up and criticize one another for not supporting Mao or the Marxist cause.

"It did not let up. I was accused of not supporting Mao because I had missed a political rally. That was the only 'crime.' But the Red Guards forced me to read a long confession of things I had never even thought of! It was a list of offenses that included owning three dress suits, giving experimental poisons to my patients, and supporting a plot to overthrow the government."

"Why didn't you defend yourself?"

"They had already made up their minds. They wanted to make an example of me. If I had resisted them I would have been beaten. As punishment, the authorities proclaimed a sentence. I am telling you these things because you are my friend. I was locked in a boarded-up room here in the hospital for several weeks with only bread and water. I couldn't take the injustice any more. I was so lonely, I just wanted to die. This was supposed to 'reeducate' us into supporting the Party! Ha! All that it did to me was to make me bitter. I support the good of my people, but I did not see that the authorities had that same idea. It was a decade of hell.

"When I think about it, I am sad. The only thing that my people learned from the Cultural Revolution was how to hate one another. They learned the futility of forced education. I have seen people made noble through suffering. I have also seen people grow bitter and apathetic. We are all healing our wounds."

Dr. Tao straightened up and wiped the sweat from his brow. "Today things are much better," he went on. "The government is more stable and we are seeing some economic progress. The great famines that used to plague China almost disappeared under the Communist Party's rule. Also, they gave us a strong army. Now we do not worry so much about the Russians attacking us. The leaders have realized that the nation needs intellectuals like me—since even they sometimes get sick. Above all, we need peace and cooperation; without these we cannot develop economically or socially. Still, there is a very bitter memory of the years of havoc and hatred. I shudder to think that it may ever happen again—not just for my own sake and my children's, but for those seven hundred patients out in the wards."

"Dr. Tao," I asked, "do you think that there is any answer for this kind of selfish evil?"

He stared toward the ceiling. "I do not know, Dr. Kong. I wish that there were!"

What's His Secret?

ONE SUNNY MORNING several weeks later, Dr. Tao and I noticed a sweet fragrance when we walked into the ward for rounds. It was quite different from the musty drab smell that winter had brought with it. Then I noticed that several varieties of chrysanthemums were sitting on a table in the room. In the pot of each there was a label that gave its name.

"We Chinese find these to be some of the most beautiful flowers," said Dr. Tao. "They all have individual names that describe them." He looked at each one for a moment, then pointed to the first. "The first one is called 'The Nobility of the People.' And next to it is 'The Glory of Productivity.' Oh, and this one, this is my favorite. This one is 'The Most Beautiful Woman in China After Her Bath.'"

The last flower had a smooth green stalk. The flower displayed multiple layers of delicate white petals. I was curious. "Why does it have this name?"

"Oh, that is easy," Dr. Tao replied. "Look at its good figure!"

As we walked on, I commented on the shirt of a student who was walking with us. "That's a cheap shirt you're wearing," I said.

"Do you mean that?" she asked.

"Oh yes, it is very cheap!"

Dr. Tao and the others looked at me in shock. Dr. Tao was appalled. "Do you know what you are saying?"

Then I remembered that the adjectives for "pretty" and "cheap" were pronounced very similarly. I corrected my mistake and we laughed.

The first patient we came to was a little girl, Feng Bei. She sat in bed with her head tilted back, looking at us through almost closed eyes. Her mother was sitting next to her. She said that Feng Bei had been a very playful child and enjoyed going to school, but this year she began to dislike going to recess with the other children. The teacher noticed her drooping eyes and she thought that the girl was just tired, so she let her stay inside. However, after several weeks she was no better, so her parents brought her to the hospital, where she had been admitted for an evaluation.

I asked Feng Bei to clap her hands together as many times as she could. I did this to test the strength of her muscles. She started with a rapid cadence, but after a moment she could hardly lift her hands. I suspected that the problem was in her nerve endings. I explained to her mother that sometimes disease causes a deficient chemical in the nerve endings. This would explain her weakness.

Next, I gave her a shot of endrophonium. It helps to increase the amount of the deficient chemical. Within minutes her strength returned. I was impressed. So was her mother. This helped to confirm the diagnosis as myesthenia gravis. I told her that in a couple of weeks she would probably be able to go back to school. At this she clapped her hands even harder.

Other patients, though, were not so eager to leave the hospital. Those who worked in a factory or on a farm continued to receive wages while they were in the hospital. Furthermore, their hospital bill was almost entirely paid for by the government. So, getting paid for not working convinced many people to stay in the hospital unnecessarily.

Doctors and hospital leaders had little authority to force them to leave. This made the situation even worse. All a patient had to do was say he did not feel well enough to go home. I cared for one middle-aged worker with a little protein in his urine who stayed on for months. Though we had explained to him many times that his disease was quite harmless, he insisted that he really was sick and would not leave until cured. For all I know, he may still be in the hospital to this day.

As we continued to go from bed to bed, we suddenly were interrupted by the arrival of several workmen carrying a young man on a stretcher. He was unconscious and his temperature was very high. As we moved him onto a bed, he had a brief convulsion. I asked a nurse to start an IV, then I turned to listen to his mother's explanation.

"It all happened so fast." Her eyes were round with fright. "When we awoke yesterday morning, my son, Chen, said he had a little headache. This kept on through the day, and last night the back of his neck started to hurt and he vomited a few times. I thought that it was just a cold, so I told him to go to bed. I came in this morning to wake him, but couldn't. He was just like he is now. Is there something I did wrong? Should I have brought him in earlier? Will he live?"

Dr. Tao took her aside to talk to her while I examined the boy. His breathing was slow and sweat covered his entire body. His neck was stiff and his eyes motionless. No reflexes were present in his arms or legs. I suspected that there was infection in his brain and spinal cord. To find out for sure, a spinal tap was quickly performed so that I could look at the fluid from around his spine and brain. It was filled with pus, which confirmed the diagnosis of meningitis. We began treating him with antibiotics given in his vein. Dr. Tao returned from talking with the boy's mother, and he and I decided to take turns watching over him for the rest of the day. It was almost noon by then and Dr. Tao wanted the first shift. I agreed to leave him for a couple of hours and made my way toward the cafeteria.

Amid the crowded hallway there was suddenly a tug at my sleeve and I turned to see Fei Chow. A young resident doctor in our department, she was the one who had congratulated me on my opera number several months earlier. She motioned me into a small linen room and closed the door. Her thin, delicate features became indistinct in the darkened room.

"Dr. Kong, I've been thinking about you for some time. You are quite handsome and bright." There was a light glow to her complexion and she blushed. "This may seem a little uncomfortable for you, but would you marry me?"

"Marry you?" I was shocked, and rather entertained. "Isn't this a little premature?"

"Well, I know that we could work things out between us and have a wonderful life. I can cook well and sew, and I can learn your language."

I crossed my arms, wondering why she would ask me such an inappropriate question. I looked at her thoughtfully. "What about your work here at the hospital? You would not want to leave it, would you?"

"Oh, that won't matter after we get to America. It will be fantastic there!"

"I have been thinking. I really like it in China. I think that I will just stay," I said. "The people are nice and the food is very good. It is better than in America."

Her expression suddenly changed. "Oh, that won't do. We must leave China and go to America as soon as possible!"

"Why do you want to marry me?"

"Because I love you!"

"Come on, what's the real reason?" I persisted. "You don't just go up to someone and ask him to marry you—at least not in China."

She began to cry. "It's this place! I can't stand to live here any more. I'm trapped in this huge impersonal system. It is so unpredictable here. I want to escape!"

"What do you mean by unpredictable?" I began to feel some genuine concern for her. "It's not so bad. You are a doctor. You have the best there is in China."

"What is right today is wrong tomorrow," she replied. "For example, we were told before that anything foreign was evil. Now the authorities invite foreigners to visit here, like you. And again, a year ago it was illegal for a person to have a private business. Now the government encourages it! Nothing is consistent. The leaders don't care for me. They won't promote me. All I do is work and go home. There is no end to it." Then her voice began to lift and there was a sparkle of hope in her eyes. "But you can help me! I understand that it is wonderful in America. But the only way I can get a passport to leave is to be your wife."

Suddenly the door opened and in walked a janitor. He looked very surprised to find us. Fei Chow continued right on speaking as we exited, "—and you see, Dr. Kong, cardiac output is equal to stroke volume times the heart rate—" Out in the hall she pulled my sleeve again and whispered to me, "Please think about it!" and quickly walked off.

"Poor lady," I thought as I went to lunch. "She is really desperate."

The dining hall was situated on the roof of the hospital building. It was crowded with a host of workers, seated thigh to thigh under low ceiling fans. At the entrance I joined the line of people, each armed with two steel bowls. One by one we filed by windows, cafeteria style. At the first, we selected from fried pork or a green vegetable. At the second window we were offered steamed dumplings and egg rolls. Whatever the choice, it was complemented by a heaping bowl of rice. The man behind me mentioned that the size of a person's body could be measured not by his weight, but by the amount of rice he could consume in one sitting. I was not sure whether or not he was joking until I got my own rice.

As I approached the window a cook asked me, "How much rice do you want?"

"Ten ounces," I replied.

"What? Ten ounces!" he said. "You must be a giant! You Americans are so large!"

I looked for a place to sit in the crowd. Previously when I did so every eye in the hall would have been on me. But now they had become used to my presence, and there was not such a scene. Some of the technicians from the X-ray department made room for me and I began to eat just the way they ate.

They mixed the greens with rice in small proportions and raised the bowl to their mouths to scoop in the mixture. A bystander stopped me for a moment to correct the hand position of my chopsticks, and the onlookers happily applauded. The tabletop was coated with a hefty layer of grease that we all did our best not to touch. The grease built up because whenever a distasteful bite of food was encountered, one simply spat it out on the table and added to the layer. Almost all of the persons sitting there had a pile of discarded inedibles on the table in front of them. When they got up from the table to leave, they simply left the inedibles behind. I had discovered that this practice is not confined to laborers and countrymen, but extended to the most intellectual physicians. I had recalled an ancient saying about Rome, but I just could not convince myself to join the practice.

After lunch came my favorite time of day. After I washed my individual utensils at a long sink, I returned them to my office. The hospital was very quiet now. Each person had gone to a personally selected part of the building for an afternoon nap. As I walked down the halls, I found a laboratory technician resting on his lab bench amid the flasks of chemicals. When I entered the ward to check on Dr. Tao, I encountered a nurse who had her head buried in her folded arms on a desk top. Dr. Tao was leaning back in his chair against the wall. He said that there had been no change in Chen. Outside, people waiting in line for the clinic had spread newspapers on the floor and were lying down. I encountered an X-ray worker asleep under his machine as I strolled along. I wondered if it was on. Content that there was little action to be missed in the upcoming hour, I, too, sought refuge in a quiet classroom and folded a newspaper across my face.

I awoke with a start and looked at my watch. Then I sat up. I still had thirty minutes to spare. In the free time before I relieved Dr. Tao, I walked back to the gastroenterology department to see some of my old patients. There was one in particular that I had wanted to talk to: Wo Wei, still in the same bed as always, looked happy to see me.

"Are you busy now? I do enjoy talking with you," he said.

"There's someone pretty sick upstairs, but I can talk for a while," I replied, pulling up a chair.

"Do you know what today is?" he asked.

"Friday."

"Correct. It is a very important day! On Friday afternoons in offices, schools, and factories all over China the work stops. The people of each work unit meet in small groups for several hours to discuss Marxist ideals and how we can build a better society."

He paused a moment, and I remembered seeing the doctors

gathering in each department on Fridays. I had overheard them discussing dialectical materialism, the dictatorship of the proletariat, and their favorite soccer stars. As the clock approached one o'clock in the afternoon, the doctors working around us filtered out of the ward to a meeting room. Attendance was mandatory.

"What are they talking about today?" I asked.

"They will be considering what kind of services the government should give to the elderly people, like free transportation and food supplements. This is upsetting to me because it misses the entire purpose of Marxism."

"What do you mean?"

"It shouldn't be the government's job to provide this. Our people should, out of the goodness of their hearts, be helping their older neighbors. Let me give you an example. This morning a man came through the ward here asking whether anyone needed his clothing washed. You know that it's almost impossible for me to do any of that for myself, so I gave him a bundle. A couple of hours later he came back with the clothes clean and folded. He wouldn't even take any money in return. Our country needs more people like him!"

Curious, I asked, "Do you remember his name?"

"I believe it was Li, Li Ming. I would like to talk with him again. He has interesting ideas!"

I was pleased that Li had struck again. "I remember that last fall you told me that once everyone is transformed or reeducated into being a New Man, the selfish elements of society will be eliminated. You also said that the need for government controls will be less and less."

"Yes, this is the theory," said Wo, "Everyone will behave so well that they won't need any control."

"But from looking at China and Russia and other Communist countries it seems that the need for a large bureaucracy and a strong military is even greater than before. Just how long has this political education process been going on? Forty years? I also have talked with several people recently who have been to the classes but have no interest at all in serving the community. Isn't there some problem with this system of reeducation?"

"Yes, yes, you have it exactly," replied Wo. "This is the critical problem. It is very difficult to change people," he said with a depressed air. "We know how to lead a revolution and establish a Marxist state. We have done this well. But to change people from ones who place self-interest first into ones who care for their neighbors—this is a key problem. Lenin had the same problem in Russia. He said, 'The workers are building the new society without having turned themselves into New Men who would be free from the dirt of the world. They are still up to their knees in it.' We have the same problem he did. Political classes don't seem to be the entire answer. I wish I knew a more effective way to change people."

"Have you ever heard about the people who built this hospital?"

"No, I have not."

"Maybe you should find out about them. The ideals that you have been teaching, however good your intentions, just aren't working very well. I bet that many of those who began this medical work were like Li Ming."

"Is that so?" Wo Wei sounded quite interested. He sat up on his bed a little. "I'll have to find out more about that man."

Just then I noticed that it was my time to watch Chen. Wo was sorry to see me go, but I assured him that I'd be back.

When I returned to the neurology ward, I found that the boy was no better. His breathing had slowed and the fever was uncontrollable. Apparently, the virus that had attacked his spinal cord and left him paralyzed had also paralyzed his breathing muscles. This made breathing even more difficult for him. I knew that if he should stop breathing, there would be nothing that we could do. If we had had a breathing machine, called a ventilator, we might have been able to save Chen's life. These machines were commonly used in America, but were scarce in China. I regretted that there was no ventilator for Chen. If he stopped breathing, he would die. I mentioned this to Dr. Tao as he left. He simply said that we would have to accept whatever happened.

Sitting next to Chen's bed, I thought of my friendship with Dr. Tao. It had taken him some time before he trusted me enough to share his thoughts. This was typical in China. Introductions to new people were always warm enough, but I could tell that people very carefully sized each other up before trusting each other. Some people attributed this to the days of the Cultural Revolution when people criticized their neighbors, their friends, and even their family to protect their own reputation as radical Maoist revolutionaries. Now they were very careful about whom they talked to.

This is interesting, I thought. *A couple of months ago I thought that I had seen a solution for injustice in society. The Marxist experiment seemed to be working here. But now I know better. They have just as many problems as we do in America.*

Chen gasped and coughed. I started to sit up, but then his breathing became smooth again and I continued my train of thought.

And then there is Li Ming. Something is remarkable about him. He has an air of friendliness and sincerity that is unmatched. I need to find out just what is in his heart. It might be the most important thing I learn in China. What is his secret?

After a couple of hours, the doctor on night duty relieved me of my watch over Chen. He was still barely clinging to life. We had done all that we could, but I did not feel good about his chances for recovery.

As I headed for the bus, I observed the people walking the streets around me. Occasionally a mother would lift her baby, no more than a year old, from her back. She would pull his pants off, then spread the baby's legs toward a tree or bush and make a hissing sound. The baby would promptly urinate. I noticed that only the small infants wore diapers. Any baby older than a year was instead subjected to this hissing performance.

"How is it," I wondered, "that these Chinese children can be trained so early, while in America it usually takes two years or more?" This began my search after one of the best-kept secrets of the Orient—toilet training.

Just then I felt a hand on my side and turned to find a wrinkled, elderly woman. It was hard to make out her speech, but I determined that she was asking me directions to a particular street. I told her what bus to go on, and then inquired, "Why did you decide to ask me, a foreigner, for directions?"

"Well, you're not really a foreigner, are you?" she replied. "You look like a man from Xinjiang Uygur."

Xinjiang is a province in Northwestern China, whose inhabitants look Caucasian. I smiled with delight that she found me so authentic looking. "Actually, I'm from Kansas City," I said, "famous for steak and baseball."

She started on her way, then turned and looked at me with a puzzled face. "Is that near the Yellow River?"

The next day I returned to find that Chen had not improved. His bed had been brought closest to the nurses' station for optimal attention. Surrounding him stood a team of doctors considering what more could be done to help him. We decided that the infection that he was suffering from was most likely polio. Dr. Tao lamented to the group that polio was a disease easily preventable by immunization. While China had one of the most successful public health programs in world history, immunization in some areas had been neglected. Chen was suffering because of this neglect.

Then a man approached us. Apparently, it was Chen's father, who had come to Shanghai that morning. He stood at the foot of the bed and began to point at his son and talk. But the words were unintelligible to me, and to everyone else in our group of twenty. We all looked at one another in frustration and asked if anyone could understand the man. When no one replied, a student left to try to find a translator. It was encouraging to me that I was not the only one who couldn't understand him.

After we finished seeing the other patients, I went down to see the little girl I had admitted earlier. Feng Bei now looked up at me through wide eyes, a sign that she was much better. Her mother was nearby, knitting her daughter a little pink shirt. I said that I was pleased with her progress and that she was responding to the medication and could go home in the morning. Then I described the previous day's scene of a mother and her urinating baby, and asked her about it.

"Oh, this practice is very common here," she said. "I had Feng Bei out of diapers by the time she was nine months old. The key is to watch the baby closely. Whenever she started to squirm a little I could tell that she was uncomfortable and probably needed to tinkle. So I just put her into position and made a hissing sound like tinkling. It did not take her long to catch on that this means go." She seemed pleased that I had asked her.

"Just a moment, let me write this down," I said. "My

friends in America would love to know about this discovery of yours! It could cause a pediatric revolution!" Then I thought, *But it would probably be socially unacceptable.*

As I closed my notebook, I noticed some activity near Chen's bed. He had stopped breathing! I walked over quickly. A nurse tried to inflate his lungs with a bag and mask, but his lungs were very stiff and she met too much resistance. I took her place and tried again. His father was watching alongside me. I put the mask tightly around Chen's mouth and squeezed the bag. I, too, could not get enough pressure to inflate his lungs. It was no use. After a moment his heart beat no more.

Instantly, the rest of his family, who had been sitting by, began to wail. I felt that same hard knot in my stomach. Since there was nothing more I could do there to help, I walked out into the hall looking for a place to rest my weak legs. I sat motionless on a bench for a few minutes, listening to their crying. I recalled what Li Ming had said: "You're a man, not some godlike figure. You're upset over the loss of a friend."

After a while, Dr. Tao came out and sat down beside me. He noticed my red face. "Dr. Kong, you don't look so well. Chen has died, but do not lose hope. There will be others whom you will be able to help."

"You are right," I replied. "I just need time to recover from the loss. We really did all that we could."

"Of course we did. Why don't we just take the afternoon off? We have to take care of ourselves sometimes you know. We can go for lunch and then take our bikes to the countryside. Too much of this work can depress me, too."

By the time the sun had reached its highest point in the sky, we were riding amid the rich green farmland surrounding

Shanghai. Across the flat fields as far as one could see there was nothing but rice and yellow oil plants waving in the wind.

As we passed a small lake, Dr. Tao pulled to a stop and led me down to the water's edge. "I want to show you something." He pointed to a group of ducks huddled along the shore and said, "This is the Yin Yang bird. Look closely and you will see that each one has a partner."

I looked at the colorful birds. They looked very happy.

"The two of them will stay together for life and even if one of them dies, the other won't take another mate," said Tao. "We call them the lovebirds. Their devotion to one another is remarkable."

"Like you and your wife?" I asked.

"Yes, indeed. In China we have a saying that marriage is like heaven on earth! This goes back for hundreds of years. There is more to our relationship with our wives than just appearances. The Tang Dynasty was particularly interesting in this regard. At that time the obese women were thought to be the most beautiful."

I was intrigued. "Did this give them any advantage over other women?" I asked.

"Oh, yes. If one was quite fat, she would likely become the wife of a landlord. So girls were encouraged to put on as much weight as possible. You see how things do change in a country as old as mine!"

We rode on to the town of Chi Bao, where we stopped to take a walk around. A market lined the edges of a shallow canal that ran through the center of the town. We bought some sugarcane and chewed the sweet wood as we strolled toward a crowd of people ahead. I was beginning to feel refreshed and grateful that Dr. Tao had suggested the trip. I had not been outside the city very often.

When we got closer to the crowd of people, I could see a

man dressed in fine clothes, standing on a box in the center of the street. He yelled in a deep voice, "The Pillow King has come to Chi Bao!" Then he began to unveil his beautiful colored silk pillowcases and comforters. Next, he raised his embroidered sheets to the onlookers, all the time saying, "Come! Make your home into a palace! Buy these fabrics and live like the emperors of old!" Dozens of people watched him perform.

I looked around to see the response. In spite of his coaxing, not a person bought one. They just stared at the precious linens and smiled at one another.

"Why don't they want these?" I asked Dr. Tao. "They look very nice."

"Just look and you'll see."

The men who stood around the Pillow King were all elderly, dressed in worn farming clothes, and chewing wheat stalks. They wore ropes as belts around their waists, and their boots were covered with mud. The answer began to dawn on me.

"They are just enjoying the show," said Tao. "None of them have any use for these things and the cost is outrageous. They are living just the way they did one hundred years ago, except that some now have TVs in their sod homes!"

We finished walking around the market and returned to find that the King had moved on. The shadows were getting long, so we unlocked our bikes and began to pedal back toward Shanghai.

We passed some swamps and rice fields as we rode. Dr. Tao stopped his bike again and sat down on a little bridge that crossed over a stream. He was looking at the water. I pulled up beside him. Near us, the water was several inches deep. Along the bushes in the water I could see some large snails crawling slowly. Several footpaths cut through the swamp toward a distant village.

"It must be hard for you to imagine," said Dr. Tao, "but here you see one of the most dangerous places in all of China. This is where the schistosomiasis larvae live."

"What are they?" I asked.

"They are tiny worms that live in water snails and penetrate the skin of people who walk through the swamps. Once inside the body, they can cause terrible damage to one's liver, lungs, and brain. In the past we didn't know how dangerous that water was—and disaster often struck. Now we know better."

I was curious as to how these little creatures could cause a disaster, so I asked him.

"There are many stories about this. One of the best known is about a town nearby called Qing Pu. One half of the people in the town died of schistosomiasis in the course of a couple of years. But then Dr. Cheng, our director, came out and helped the people fight the worms."

"How did they do it?" I asked, looking at the murky water. It did not look so dangerous, but I did not want to get any on myself.

"They drained the swamps and filled the ponds with dirt. Then they dug new wells for water and built homes away from the infested area. Now the town is safe. A lot of people consider public health work like this pretty boring, but it's far easier to prevent this disease than to treat it. The town is an example for all of us in China."

My thoughts returned to the hospital, and the lump came back to my throat. I added, "Kind of like immunizing people against polio?"

"Yes, you are right," replied Dr. Tao. "The people of Qing Pu got a second chance on life. They got to start over again." He paused a moment, as if thinking of something else. Then a smile came to his face. "Wouldn't it be great if we could just forget all of these political conflicts and just leave the old way of life behind? Dr. Kong, wouldn't it be great if we could all have a new life?"

"It certainly would!" I replied. "The efforts to change people here have failed. We do need a new start."

"But where," asked Dr. Tao, "can the power to start again come from?" He looked toward the skyline. "Where can it come from?"

chapter six

What to Do?

I HAD AN APPOINTMENT for dinner, but the evening began with chaos and confusion. It started with explosions that echoed through the dark buildings. I climbed onto the roof to see what was happening. In the streets, bands of workers were marching. Sparks flew behind them and volleys of shots echoed in the alleys. I wondered what was happening. Rockets jetted through the sky, exploding into brilliant colors. Below me, children ran yelling to their parents. From the roof I saw men sharpening their long knives. Cars raced by, horns blowing. Ash filled the air as cannons fired in the distance. Soldiers stood in the streets while women scurried home lugging provisions.

Back inside the dorm, the students on my floor madly threw a few clothes into their handbags and abandoned the building. "What is going on?" I called out, but no one replied. They had all left. Even the doorkeeper had left his post. Wasting no time, I grabbed a coat and entered the night. Bombs fell on the streets and exploded with a deafening roar. Men raced by on their bicycles. There were pools of blood on the sidewalks.

"Are the Russians invading?" I asked a bystander.

"No!" came his reply. "It is Chinese New Year!"

"Oh, so that's it! I thought there was a battle starting!" I felt better. I had been warned about the festivities, but it still was not what I had expected.

I arrived at Dr. Cheng's home just in time to see him and his sons set off the last of their fireworks.

"Dr. Kong, you're late!" called out the aging hospital director.

"Sorry. I was surprised by all the excitement. It was more than I had expected!"

"They are excited with good reason!" said Dr. Cheng, "These three days are the longest break people here ever get. It is the most important holiday in all of China."

We walked inside his spacious four-room home. An ancient piano stood in one corner. After pouring us glasses of cool rice wine, Dr. Cheng led me to seats on the balcony, where we watched the festivities.

"You really are a privileged man, Dr. Kong," he said as he sat down. "You have had the opportunity to see firsthand the social progress of our country. We are proud of the strides that have been made. How do you think it compares with America?"

"Honestly, sir?"

"Of course. Go ahead and speak your mind."

Six months earlier I would have been hesitant to answer a question like this. But I knew now that he was sincere. "I really think that the Chinese people still struggle from the same basic problems as we do in America. I really can't see much difference in them except for the outward structure of society."

Dr. Cheng seemed undaunted. "Well, you are not looking hard enough. You can, of course, see that there are no distinct classes of people in China today. They all make the same amount of money. This is one area of success for us."

"I do have one question about this 'classless' society." I knew that it might be a touchy subject, but I felt I should ask. "Why is it that the Party members that I know have better homes than most? And why is it that they have special cars on the train? Why do their children—"

Here Cheng interrupted. "Kong, they need these things so that they can carry out their leadership responsibilities. They need to be rested and well cared for if they are to care for the country. Just look at the president of your country. Would he accept less?"

"No, he would not," I answered. He got me on that one!

Cheng's wife came out and sat down beside him. I did not think that she spoke English, but I decided that we'd talked enough about politics anyway.

"What kinds of things do people do to celebrate the New Year?" I asked.

"Because our ancient calendar is different, we celebrate the New Year now, in February, unlike you Westerners. But the actual preparations for the holiday began long beforehand. My wife started to put aside money for our feast months ago. Then she went to the markets to find the mushrooms and the rare fish that make our dinners so special. One of the final steps is slaughtering the chickens. This is what I did outside last night."

"Oh, I had wondered where all the blood came from!" I laughed. "Do you visit friends on this holiday?"

"We have a custom that deals with this also," Dr. Cheng explained. "On the first day of the festival everyone goes to the home of his family for a dinner party. My three sons came over this morning and spent the day. Then, on the second day, you visit your professors or labor chief. You're a day early, Kong!"

"Next year I'll have it straight," I said.

"Finally, on the last day, we meet our friends. Usually we just talk about old times until late at night," he said with a yawn. He stretched out on the sofa on his porch.

"If a young man goes to the home of his girlfriend on New Year's, it is a sign that they will become engaged. If you want to know who is close to marriage, just ask them where they spent New Year's." A skyrocket roared overhead, but Dr. Cheng didn't even flinch.

I sipped the sweet wine and wondered how they could have ever had a New Year without fireworks.

"Who started the holiday?" I asked.

"No one really knows for sure," said Dr. Cheng, now staring off toward the blitzkrieg on the horizon. "It has gone on since historians began writing. Years ago it was called the Harvest Festival. The peasants would rest for a few days and enjoy eating what they had grown."

His eyes were growing more heavy as we continued to talk. His wife began to yawn and went inside. She shut off the lights in the house.

"Now, we like these days just to remember our past and see . . ." The sentence was never finished, and I looked over to see the stately Dr. Cheng sleeping, his head back against the sofa.

What amazing things this man has to remember, I thought. *He has watched China come from a feudal, backward land, through wars and revolutions, to become a world power. What an awesome privilege!* I stepped over the slumbering figure and made my way down to the street and back to my vacant dormitory. Dr. Cheng was right: I did have a lot to learn.

A volley of bottle rockets roused me from bed the next morning. As I made my way along the streets, the aroma of a thousand kitchens hung in the breeze. Women were sitting at tables in front of their small homes. They were busy dicing vegetables, or sewing, or just talking in groups. One man was folding colored paper into a pinwheel for his starry-eyed daughter. On a street corner stood an old gentleman, clad in fading gray coveralls, blowing up balloons from a hydrogen tank. Children crowded around to buy them and giggled whenever a balloon exploded because of the glowing cigarette in the man's mouth!

As the morning sun slowly became visible, I walked into a little park in the center of the city. Two sculptures of long dragons formed the low wall that stretched around the park. Their heads were mounted to guard each side of the gate. When I walked in, I saw two elderly couples with swords at their sides standing in a small courtyard. I paused a moment to watch them dance. They men whirled their weapons in the air, then the women joined in with a graceful step, and all jumped as if to a silent melody. Near me, a young artist painted the dancers into her scene. Along the walls a dignified-looking man was leading his young disciples in the martial arts, but he noticed the couples and abruptly brought his pupils to a halt. He looked toward the dancers and I heard him say, "They are beautiful!"

The couples held hands, exchanged smiles, and then slowly twirled their swords back to their sides. They bowed to one another in their finale, hardly seeming to notice that they had attracted the attention of everyone in the park. We all gave them a silent applause. They represented a culture so deep and rich I couldn't help but stand in awe. In spite of all their hard work, they took time to express and preserve their traditions.

Too quickly the taste of history was over. After the busy holidays came the drudgery of Monday morning. Back to work for the tired multitudes. To add to the gloom on this particular day, the city was covered by fog so thick one could barely see five yards. It was too dangerous to ride my bicycle, so I joined the workers waiting at the bus stops. We stood and talked and looked at our watches. No bus. I pulled out my little book and reviewed my vocabulary words. Still no bus. Frustration grew as the minutes became an hour, then two hours, and no buses could be seen.

I went up to a man next to me and asked, "What do you think the problem is?"

"Perhaps the drivers wanted to sleep in a day extra for the holiday," he said. "Besides, they will get paid the same whether they work or not."

"What will my boss say?" said one.

Another answered, "He's probably late too—don't worry!"

Then I began to notice men walking down the street. First one, then a few. Before long there were gangs of laborers walking into the city. "The trolleys aren't running!" they shouted. "The drivers refused to work in the fog!" With sighs, we joined their ranks. Soon there were thousands of us marching through the narrow, winding thoroughfares, under the overhanging verandas. One mile, two miles, three, four. It was like a grand parade, although no one was smiling. As I arrived at the Rei Jing Hospital, the fog suddenly cleared and the sun broke through. When I walked through the gate, the first public bus drove by.

Before me were the beautiful gardens of the largest hospital in all of Asia. It was associated with the Third People's Hospital, and I had been asked to come to visit for a day. Made up of more than a dozen brick buildings spread over several acres, Rei Jing looked more like a college campus than a hospital. Each building housed a different department and was connected to the others by walkways lined with bushes and flower beds. In the center of the complex I passed a fish pond filled with huge goldfish. A healing spirit of peace and contentment prevailed over the courtyards—in glaring contrast with the urban sprawl surrounding the Third Hospital. I enjoyed the change.

I walked until I found the building that read "Nei Kuh," meaning internal medicine. Dr. Jiang Wei, chief of the internal medicine department, met me in his small office and greeted me in French. He noticed my frustrated look, then spoke in perfect English. "Forgive me, Dr. Kong. You see, I was trained in Paris before coming back to China fifty years ago. I was not sure which language you spoke. I'm happy to have this opportunity to meet you. This morning I'll be lecturing the students here. We will be talking about some of the basic principles underlying Chinese traditional medicine. Dr. Cheng called me and thought it essential that you learn something about this during your time in China."

"I'm sure that many people back home will think I am an expert in it after I return," I remarked. Already, I had been receiving letters from people asking me questions about acupuncture.

"Perhaps," he said, "but it takes years of study to understand traditional medicine. I can only offer you some introduction."

We walked to a small conference room where a few students were seated on wooden benches. Each was armed with a glass of hot tea and a pen to record the lecture.

As he spoke, Dr. Jiang showed slides on an ancient projector. I noticed that he looked particularly handsome and well-kept for an elderly man. I also noticed that he, too, had large ears!

"One of the fundamental principles you must grasp is that of yin and yang," he said. "This is based on the concept that everything in the body must be kept in balance to avoid disease. If there is too much yin, for example, or too little yang, then one will likely become sick.

"The classic example of applying this theory to modern medicine can be seen in the function of the thyroid gland in the neck. This gland secretes a very important hormone, but a balance must be kept. If too much thyroid hormone is secreted, the person often loses weight, sweats, and has a fast pulse rate. We could say that he has too much yin. If too little thyroid hormone is secreted into the body, a person may become overweight, tired, and have a slow pulse. This represents an excess of yang."

Here, he paused a moment to allow the point to settle in.

"Dr. Jiang, how long has this concept of yin and yang been known?" I asked.

"For several thousand years, Dr. Kong. It is a fascinating thing that ancient people were able to discover these principles without any equipment but their keen observations. It was not until the 1900s that Western medicine discovered this concept of balance in the body's hormones.

"As you know, today we can treat thyroid disease with modern drugs. For instance, if there is too little thyroid hormone, we give the patient some extra hormone to take orally. The thing that is most important for you to note, however, is that there are also traditional medicines that can increase the amount of yin and yang in the body."

Here I sat up. If these drugs that he spoke of actually could change the amount of hormones in a person, they might really have some use back home.

He continued, "A person with a deficiency of thyroid hormone has too much yang and too little yin, so we give them an herb known to increase the yin in the body. The function of their thyroid may then return to normal even without giving extra thyroid hormones by mouth."

Here I interrupted again. None of the students dared to ask him a question, so I had free rein. "Dr. Jiang, this concept of balancing yin and yang seems to apply pretty well to thyroid disease, but what about other diseases?"

"Other endocrine diseases, like diabetes and Cushing's disease, fit this theory well," he explained. "However, heart disease and neurologic disease often do not fit the concepts I just presented. But there are other theories of Chinese traditional medicine that can explain them better."

He then discussed how in Chinese medicine there are five components to the body: wood, water, air, fire, and earth. An excess or deficiency of any of these five components can cause disease if not corrected. It reminded me of the ancient Greek understanding of medicine, which has several similar components.

He concluded, "It is important for you not to become bound by the concepts of traditional medicine as the answer to all the health problems that you face. Instead, these concepts must be combined with what is known today to give the most benefit to our patients. You need to avoid being too radical in your approach."

As our meeting broke up, I approached the professor.

"Dr. Jiang, I'd like to ask you a personal question, if you don't mind." He nodded to me, so I continued, "You look so healthy, and your mind is so quick. Yet, you said that you went to Paris in 1917. How old are you?"

He laughed and there was a sparkle in his eye. "I'm eighty-nine years old now. But I feel as if I were forty-five! It has been wonderful to live and see so much."

"I've met several people like you in China who live such long, full lives," I said. "What is the secret? There must be something that you have done to be so well-kept."

"The answer," he replied, "is everything in moderation.

Not too much studying or sleeping late. Not too much alcohol or good food, nor too much crying or laughing. Keep everything in balance. This is the key."

"Kind of like balancing yin and yang?" I asked.

"Precisely!"

Still, I was not satisfied. "But surely there is something more," I persisted. "Some mystery buried in ancient history."

He held his chin with one hand and was silent for a moment, thoughtfully staring off into space.

"There is something else," he said. I looked up at him with anticipation. "This was discovered by the great philosophers of ancient China," he said with a smile—"You must play badminton every day." His words echoed down the great hall and his pupils scribbled down his quote for their own longevity. "Badminton is refreshing to the mind and soul. I invite you to come to a park with me someday and play."

"I'd like that very much. Perhaps I could prescribe this for my patients as well," I suggested, and he agreed with a definitive nod.

In the late afternoon I returned to the Third Hospital. A severely crippled young man stood in front watching over a long row of black bicycles. He and his mother were the ones who usually kept mine while I was inside. The halls were much more quiet now in the evening. The visitors were not yet allowed inside. One could hear the faint scratching of metal plates as patients ate with chopsticks. In the ward a man stopped to ask me how the opera singer was doing. I told him that he had gone home several weeks before. He may be performing opera again by now.

Then I noticed Zhange, the artist who had leukemia. He had his blankets pulled close to his chin and looked weak and pale. I was not surprised to find Li Ming, looking rather thin himself, sitting next to his bed. Li slowly raised bits of

steaming rice from a bowl into the air to cool, a small cloud of
mist forming above each morsel before it was fed into the
artist's open mouth. He would chew for a moment, and then
rest before swallowing the rice.

Wo Wei lay nearby. "The artist is not well," he said.

"What is the problem?" I asked.

"During the Spring Festival he began to vomit. It's kept up
for days. Poor man. The nurses tried to feed him something
because it had been so long since he had kept anything down,
but they do not have enough time to spend with him—there
are so many other jobs they have to do. I was getting worried
that Zhange would starve."

"It's terrible to think that someone would starve in a
hospital, but it happens in America, too."

"A couple of nights ago, Li Ming, the peasant over there,
came in and asked the nurses if they needed any help. All of
them pointed toward the artist. Every evening since then Li
has come here to feed him!"

"That is amazing," I said.

Wo Wei looked back at me. "So, Kong, you are late
coming. What did you do all day?"

"I went to a lecture over at Rei Jing Hospital. It really is a
lovely place—all those flower gardens and trees. So different
from the crowded streets around our hospital."

"Yes, it's a tremendous problem."

"What's that? All the flower gardens?"

"No. All the people, of course," said Wo. "This is the
biggest problem we have in China. Taking care of them is
almost more than we can handle. It was not always that way."

"How did there get to be so many people?"

"It started soon after Chairman Mao led the party. He
thought that if we had more people, this meant more
manpower and therefore, greater production. So, people were

encouraged to have as many children as possible. This was to increase the work force.

"The problem is that all these new people need houses and food. They need clothes and education. We don't have the resources to provide this for a billion people."

"It is a huge task," I agreed. "Surely there is some way to make the job easier. How does the Party expect to deal with this?"

"The answer is to control the population," replied Wo Wei. "Fewer people means more for everyone, so we encourage couples to marry later. According to our laws they can have only one child. If every family has only one baby, then after another twenty or thirty years our population will begin to level off. Even if everyone has only one, the population will still increase to about one and a quarter billion before we see a slowdown. This is optimistic, though, for some people, especially those in the country, want to have more than one."

I thought a moment before replying. "Imagine that," I said, "an entire culture with only one child per family. That means no brothers or sisters, no uncles or aunts, no nieces or nephews or cousins. What happens if a woman becomes pregnant a second time?"

"Well, we try to prevent that with contraceptives," said Wo, "but if she is pregnant again, she will almost always have an abortion."

"What!" I exclaimed.

"Yes. The only real option is to have an abortion. If she insists on keeping her second baby, there is a very heavy fine. The family must pay for the child's health care and education. Normally these are provided at no charge for the first child. It's more than almost anyone can afford to pay, so they just have abortions. This is necessary. If my country is too large, we cannot grow economically. Besides, most women don't mind having an abortion if it is for the good of the country."

We paused a moment and I noticed Li Ming washing up the artist's eating bowls by a sink. He walked over, placed them in a cabinet, and waved a farewell to the two of us as he left the ward.

"There are many people dedicated to keeping down the population," Wo continued. "Let me tell you a story about one. Each province of China has a department to enforce the birth control policy. In the countryside one of these departments had a woman whose job it was to go to the factories and farms and lecture about the need for population control. She showed the workers how to use contraception. She was a zealous person and many paid attention to her instructions.

"She was a lovely woman, but she and her husband were not able to have children themselves, though they had tried for years. Finally they had lost all hope of having their own child, so they went to the adoption office and took a baby who had no parents. They really loved their new baby and took him for all the neighbors to see. Everyone was so happy that their wish had come true. And all the time she continued her work of promoting the one-family, one-child policy.

"But then after a couple of years she became pregnant! Her husband was very happy, for this would be a child of their very own, but she was in great distress. She already had one child, and she had been teaching the people to have only one. Now she was going to have two children! This would mean a setback for the country. It would mean going back on all that she had worked for. How could she ever speak to people about one child when she had two? What to do?" At this, Wo paused and looked around the room to let his message sink in to those who were listening to us talk.

"Well, what happened?" I asked.

"That brave woman," said Wo, "went to the hospital and aborted the baby. What courage! What dedication! We will control the population!"

He looked at me for a sign of approval. I returned only a stare of utter disgust. He did not say anything more. He looked down at his feet. Those who had been listening just turned around.

I sensed that Wo had caught himself in his own story. After a moment, I spoke. "Wo, is it worth it? You know that it isn't! The idea to create a perfect society by propaganda and rules is not working! Look what it is producing: a generation of unhappy, untrusting people. Look at what it is costing— thousands of lives." This time, I paused to let it sink in.

After several silent moments he said in a quiet voice, "You are right." He was still looking at his feet. "You're right. It is not working." His voice was tense with emotion. He looked up at me. "But, Dr. Kong, I do not know any other way! I just do not know what else to do. We have tried several systems of government and philosophy before, and nothing works very well."

"Have you heard of any other way to deal with society?" I asked.

His eyes brightened somewhat. "Yes, I have. Li Ming and I talked just today when he came in. He has some strange ideas about how people can get along with one another. By looking at him, I'd say that he may have some good points. I am going to read more about it all."

At this he lifted up a small black book from his night stand. "Li loaned it to me for a few days. I am going to read the entire thing. I'll let you know what I find!"

The New Man

*W*ANG EDGED HIS WAY UPWARD along the bamboo scaffolding surrounding an ancient pagoda in Shanghai's southwest corner. The long poles, rising 150 feet into the air, enclosed the tall, round structure like a huge cage. The pagoda had been built in the 1200s and was a sacred place to the Buddhists. Seven balconies extended from the building, and a long, circular staircase inside wound around toward the tower at the very top.

Sitting on the dirty scaffolding, Wang and his companions were slowly replacing the rotting wood and painting the structure a bright yellow. They had to balance themselves carefully as they worked on the thin poles that supported them. As he leaned to dip his brush, Wang suddenly slipped backwards. His friends looked up just in time to see his feet disappear over the edge of the scaffolding.

While they gasped in horror, Wang fell, crashing into the poles thirty feet below them, splintering wood and snapping ropes with the impact of his fall. The workers let out a shout and quickly climbed down to find him suspended on his stomach over a cracked pole a hundred feet above the ground.

They eased the broken man through a window and carried him down the staircase. There was no telephone for blocks, so one of them stopped a man who was riding a three-wheeled bicycle. The small platform in back of the three-wheeler served as a bed for Wang. Here they laid him gently down and pedaled off into the city with all speed.

In another part of town I stood with an elderly man from New Zealand. I had just picked him up from the airport on my way to work. He had come to visit Keith, who was going to meet us at the hospital gate. We were waiting with perhaps a hundred others for a bus to arrive. As it stopped, I stationed the two of us in front of the door and let the crowd behind us push my friend and me on board—a useful technique I had learned months before. It was very crowded on the bus, and a Chinese man offered his seat to the New Zealander, who graciously accepted.

Once the Chinese man was standing, I noticed that he was very tanned and fit. "How old are you?" he asked my New Zealand friend in good English.

"I'm sixty-four years old," said my friend, gasping for breath after the bus-boarding experience. "I can barely get around anymore. You sure look fine. How old are you?"

"I'm eighty-one!" said the man.

"What!" exclaimed the New Zealander. "You should be sitting here!" He began to get up, but the Chinese man insisted that he keep his seat. I could not help but chuckle at their little argument.

Just then our bus arrived at the hospital gate. Keith boarded the bus and wondered what the discussion was all about. I got off, leaving the three of them to debate who should get the seat.

Spring had come with its sunny days, and I had begun to work in the surgery department, where I would spend my last three months in China. As I walked to the operating room that morning, I was met by one of the surgeons, Dr. Shi.

"Kong, remember the man with the hernia that you were going to operate on this morning? Well, we need to postpone him until later. A man just came in who fell out of a pagoda. I examined him, and I believe that he is bleeding internally."

"He fell out of a what?" I exclaimed.

"A pagoda," repeated Dr. Shi.

"I have heard of people falling from windows, and from trucks," I said, "but never a pagoda."

Dr. Shi was not amused. "Dr. Kong, remember, this is China. Now get dressed."

In the surgery lounge I selected the largest scrub clothes I could find. Still, the shirt fit like a mold across my chest and the pants were a foot too short around my ankles. I put my street clothes in a locker and hung the key around my neck. One of the other surgeons noticed my plight.

"We're not used to having surgeons built as large as you!" he exclaimed. I looked up and recognized him. Just a week before I had watched him operate and remove an infected appendix from his own son. I had noticed that he tied a lot more knots in the sutures than were usually necessary. I would probably have done the same.

The most difficult part of getting ready was to find a fitting pair of special sandals to wear into the operating room. We wore these so that we would not track dirt from outside. They were all made of rubber and invariably left my heels hanging out the back to rub the floor. Occasionally I could not find any that would fit at all. Then I had no choice but to operate barefoot. Soon, I had earned the nickname "Big Barefoot Doctor."

Wang was being put to sleep when I entered the operating room. His blood pressure was very low, indicating that he had lost a serious amount of blood. I hurried to scrub my hands with Dr. Shi at a large sink in the room. Above the sink in faded paint was a slogan by Chairman Mao: "Serve the people."

Wang's skin had already been sterilized by the circulating nurse, so I placed the drapes about his abdomen. My heart began to pound as I incised his abdomen in the middle. I did not know just what injuries I might find, which added to the anticipation. When I had opened his abdomen, blood began to pour out from everywhere. We hurried to suction it all into a bottle and infuse it back into his veins like a transfusion, for there was still no blood in the blood bank.

Once most of the blood was out of the way, we looked around and discovered that the bleeding was coming from his torn spleen. I put a large clamp across the base of the organ. The profuse bleeding stopped immediately and I breathed a sigh of relief.

His blood pressure began to rise after a few moments. I looked around the rest of his abdomen, but could not find any other injuries. I then returned to the spleen and began to repair it with a series of silk sutures. Dr. Shi looked on approvingly.

"Dr. Shi," I asked, "there are several kinds of sutures, like nylon, gut, and steel. Why do you always like to use silk?"

"Oh, that's easy," he replied. "This is China. We have lots of silk here. What would you expect?"

"It seems reasonable to me."

"Dr. Kong," he asked while we worked, "do you know the proverb about traveling?"

"No, not that one," I replied. It seemed that there was a proverb for everything!

"The proverb says that when you go somewhere, be sure to leave something behind." He paused and I looked into Wang's open abdomen. "But do not do this in surgery!" He laughed, and I made sure that we indeed had not. The two of us worked quickly to close his abdomen with layers of suture. After another twenty minutes, Wang was in the recovery room.

After the operation I went to the men's surgery ward. It was lined with thirty beds in two long rows. Patients sat beside the beds reading newspapers or playing cards. One very old man with only one tooth jutting out of his mouth held a large magnifying glass and scanned the room. He was startled when I came into his view.

A pretty nurse sat beside her father, who was too weak to sit up by himself. His face was deeply jaundiced. We had discovered the week before that he suffered from gall bladder cancer. Sadly, the chance of recovery was nil. His hands trembled. She gently touched his arm to calm his anxiety and a tear ran down her face. Lifting a damp cloth, she wiped the sweat from his brow and tried to feed him some porridge.

After a while I heard some loud hiccups coming from the recovery room next door. When I arrived, I found Wang awake and violently hiccuping. Dr. Shi and I were both aware that this was a dangerous situation after surgery, and could cause the incision in his abdomen to reopen.

"In traditional American medicine, how do you treat this?" Shi asked quickly.

"It's an art developed and tested over centuries," I replied. "We call it the paper bag!"

We found one at the bedside of another patient and put it to work. Unfortunately, it did not make any difference, and Wang's abdominal pain became more and more severe.

"It's my turn," said Dr. Shi. "It is time for Chinese traditional medicine!" With a flourish, he pulled two needles from his pocket and pierced Wang's ears with them. Within minutes his hiccups ceased! I was impressed.

Wang, in his somnolent state, congratulated Dr. Shi. He

added, "America is much too young a country to have any really effective medicines!"

Unfortunately, illness and injuries were not confined to daylight hours alone. The six doctors in our department took turns staying at the hospital at night to care for those needing attention. So, one night a week I stayed at the hospital. I had a bed in my office, where the nurses would come to get me up when I was needed.

The dark halls and quiet wards were usually peaceful at night, unlike many American hospitals. I had time to talk with people. But, at least once a night, a nurse would find me and announce, "Lan wei yen," meaning there was a new patient with appendicitis.

One night we decided to operate in the extra operating room under the hospital. It was used for more minor procedures. Actually, it was in an old underground bomb shelter that now housed more than fifty patients. A boy with appendicitis had already been brought down there from the emergency room, so Dr. Shi and I entered through the small vaultlike door and descended a narrow staircase into the series of concrete tunnels. At the end of one of these catacombs was the operating room. We entered it through another vaultlike door. Here, a lone light hung above the bare operating table. A table near the wall held the sterilized instruments.

The frightened young boy was sitting in a wheelchair. His thin body was tense with pain, and all the activity around him did not help. The anesthesiologist arrived and laid him on the table. While he was being put to sleep, I looked for some way to make myself useful.

"Kong, would you plug in the operating lamp?" asked Dr. Shi. I went to do so, but the plug and the socket in the wall didn't match. "Try using one of those adaptors," said Shi. I tried several different sizes from a box in the room. But none of the six adaptors fit the lamp plug. As I searched around the bomb shelter, I discovered that none of the other sockets fit the plug either, so returned to the operating room.

"Hopeless," I said to him.

"It's a very common problem," he replied. "There are no standard plugs or socket sizes in China. Instead, there are a dozen or more different kinds. This causes constant confusion." He looked a little frustrated.

Instead, we found a portable light. It was not as bright, but it was better than working in the dark. The boy was now asleep, and the operation got under way smoothly. I stood in my rubber sandals at the right of the boy. Dr. Shi was on the left. A tired medical student handed us the instruments. He yawned several times while we worked. The clock read 3:30 in the morning. When I removed the red, swollen appendix, I handed it toward the student. He had his eyes closed. So I asked Dr. Shi, "How do you feel about making students work all night like this?"

"He needs the experience! We have an ancient Chinese saying about this." Then in exquisite Chinese he said: "No pain, no gain!"

Sounds like something my coach would say, I thought.

After the operation was completed, we carried the boy to his room in another part of the shelter. On the way over, Dr. Shi received a phone call and quickly left without explaining why. So, after the boy was in bed, I attempted to find my way above ground. I hoped to sleep a couple of hours before morning. I walked down a long corridor, looking for the main door. I turned some corners and was soon lost in the pitch-black darkness. I groped along the walls, trying to find my way back from where I had come. I felt for a door or a light switch, but there was nothing around but dust. I was becoming frustrated.

Then I stumbled across a pipe on the floor. I lost my balance and struck my chest as I fell. I rested a moment on the ground, my chest throbbing, but then I saw a glimmer of light. It was from a hatch leading upward. I got up and crawled on my hands and knees toward it. There was a small ladder nearby, and I climbed up and peered out through a little window. Using all the force I could muster, I shoved against the hatch. It made my chest hurt, but the latch didn't budge an inch.

"What a life," I thought. "From a small college town in Missouri, to die lost in a dungeon of Shanghai." After more searching in the dark, I returned to the hatch. I had the pipe with me this time and I used it to smash open the little window. I began to shout for help through the hole. I called several times, but no response. Then I tried calling again. This went on for what seemed like half an hour. Finally, fatigue overcame me and I lay down on the ground, exhausted.

But someone must have heard my calls, for after several more minutes I heard some footsteps. They grew louder, and then I saw a light. My heart lifted. A man rounded the corner with a lantern. It was the father of the boy I had just operated on!

"Dr. Kong!" he said with a laugh, "I thought I heard someone calling. You rescued my son, and now it's my turn to return the favor."

"Am I glad to see you! Show me to the bed."

He led me back to the entrance of the shelter and I climbed the narrow staircase. The hospital grounds looked different at night, so quiet and serene, in striking contrast to the drama that was lived out there each day.

The following morning, in spite of my great fatigue, I went about the ward seeing those patients whom we had operated

on the day before. I was startled to find Wo Wei lying on a
bed in the surgery department.

"When did you come here?" I asked.

"Early this morning," he replied anxiously. "My colon
disease had been acting up, and I began to pass blood
yesterday. The doctors have not been able to control it and
decided they will need to operate this morning in order to
save me." He clutched the rail of the bed.

"When are they going to do it?" I asked. I was in shock
myself over his sudden turn for the worse. Neither of us had
expected this.

"About now." He glanced at the door. "In fact, this may be
my nurse coming to get me."

"How do you feel?"

"I'm scared to death," he replied, shaking his head. "I
always felt secure in my thinking, but not now. The ideology
that I have lived for is a failure. My body is a failure. It's all
crashing in on me!" His face was full of sweat and drawn up
tight. "I believe, Dr. Kong, that Li Ming is right."

"What do you mean by that?" I asked. I took hold of his
arm. "Right about what?"

"About the message that he told me, about new life. I think
that he is right. I must talk to him again!"

The nurse reached us, pushing a cart from the operating
room up to his bed. She began to lift his frail body over on to
it.

Wo Wei looked at me, with a pleading look. "Dr. Kong, if
I die, I want you to find out—"

The nurse cut him short, "Now don't you be talking like
that!" She hung his IV bottle on a pole and began to push the
cart away. Suddenly there was a call from the doorway.

"Wait a moment!"

The three of us looked up to see Li Ming walking quickly toward us.

"Wo, I heard that you were worse and I came over as quickly as I could."

Wo's forlorn eyes held a ray of hope in them. He gazed up at Li. "My friend, you remembered me also."

There was silence in the ward. A group of men who were watching put down their cards. Some doctors set aside their charts, to see what would happen. "Look at that big shot," said one, "yelping like a puppy. He ruled over us, but now he's getting what he deserves!"

Li came close and spoke to Wo in a deep, tender voice. "I know the fear. I've been there, too. Remember this, Wo—my family and I, we care for you! But what's more, God does also. Nothing can change that. I'll stand by you through this. You can depend on it!"

Wo began to smile, and a tear danced in his eyes. "I know, Li. You are right!"

The nurse, anxious to finish her task, had had enough. She motioned Li aside and rolled Wo toward the door. He looked back at us. There was more hope in his eyes than before.

Li and I watched until he was out of sight. Then I turned toward him. "What is it about you, Li? Why do you care for him and these others? I mean, you don't have to come here and help them. You're not well yourself!"

"Well, Dr. Kong, these people need help. Some of them, like Wo Wei, hardly have any friends at all, and this can be a very lonely place."

"But you have a family and work to do also," I said. "You're different. You seem to have so much peace and security. You're not like most of the people here. You are not like the workers that I have seen. You have real courage. Where does it come from?"

"Thank you, Dr. Kong. I'll show you!" he said.

He reached into the rice sack he was carrying and pulled out the small black book. He flipped the pages for a second. Finding a place, he began to read in Chinese.

"Rejoice in the Lord always. I will say it again: Rejoice! Let your gentleness be evident to all. The Lord is near. Do not be anxious about anything, but in everything, by prayer and petition, with thanksgiving, present your requests to God. And the peace of God, which transcends all understanding, will guard your hearts and your minds in Christ Jesus."

He closed the book and looked up at me. "Dr. Kong, this is the secret of my life. I believe in Jesus Christ. He has changed my entire life. I can love Wo and these others because I know the greater love. It is the love that only Jesus can give."

I felt relieved inside. I also felt guilty. "Li," I said, "I also am a Christian. But until I met you I never realized how much power our faith can give us to show goodness to others!"

"Thank you, Dr. Kong. But you see, it is Jesus Christ working through me. It is indeed wonderful. It is the secret to peace and prosperity for everyone."

A couple of weeks later I was in the ward again talking with Wo Wei. His surgery had been successful and the bleeding had stopped. Wo looked tired, but relieved.

"I never really knew what it was like to suffer before this," he said. "There were days when I thought I'd never walk out of here again. You know that Li Ming—he continued to visit for several days after my operation. Each time, we both read from his book and then talked about it. I want to find out more about his faith. He even fed me a couple of times when I felt weak. But I haven't seen him in a few days. Do you know where he is?"

I looked at the ground, and my hands began to sweat. "Wo, I have something I need to tell you." I paused, trying to think of the right words. "Yesterday, they carried Li into the hospital from his sister's home. He had a bad fever. His heart wasn't working well." I paused for a moment. Wo was looking at me intensely. "I was with him when he slipped away."

Wo sat up with a jolt. "No!" he shouted. "No! No!" he said more loudly. "How could we lose him?" He paused, and then lay back down. "I mean, he had the answer!"

"I'm sorry, too. I don't understand," I said.

Wo Wei was quiet for what seemed like an hour. He was looking down, staring at his feet. His gray hair waved in the breeze passing through the ward. After a moment the breeze died down and Wo turned to me. His words were firm.

"He was the New Man."

chapter eight

The New Community

D R. SHI AND I WERE UP to our arms in work. For the entire day we had been operating on a man with colon cancer. The tumor had spread to much of his abdomen, and yet it seemed possible to remove a large part of it, so we painstakingly continued to cut away the tumor. The room was cold from the air conditioner and my feet were getting sore. At one point, we took a break and drank hot milk from a straw that the circulating nurse put around our masks so that we could remain sterile. Dr. Shi took the opportunity to comment on my performance that morning.

"Dr. Kong, you tie knots very well. Better than a month ago."

I was surprised at his compliment, for he was usually quite businesslike. "Thank you, Dr. Shi. It comes from lots of experience 'serving the people,'" I said.

He looked back at me. "Do you really mean that—about serving the people?"

"Of course I do," I replied. "I am for China. I want to see this man, and all Chinese, have a good life."

"That is a refreshing attitude," he replied. "I thought that you were just here to make a name for yourself. Isn't it true that most Americans are like that, just out to take care of themselves?"

We sat down on separate stools, careful so as not to become

contaminated. I responded to his question cautiously. "I know that you have heard some bad things about Americans, but most of them are people just like you, who want to have a peaceful life. They want to have families and excel in their work. You would find them quite kind."

"Dr. Kong, if they are all like you, then we should have no conflict at all. Now let's go back to work."

He got up and walked back to the table. I followed, realizing that this was perhaps the most meaningful compliment I had received since I had been in China.

After completing the surgery in the evening, I went to see Wo Wei. It had been three weeks since his operation and he looked much better. When I came in, he was sitting up beside his bed reading from Li Ming's Bible. His radio was on, the volume turned a little higher than it should have been. He noticed me walk in.

"Dr. Kong, it is good to see you again!" He was clearly a happy man. "Look at what I am reading here. It says here that 'if anyone is in Christ, he is a new creation; the old has gone, the new has come!' Doesn't that sound familiar?"

"It does," I replied. "It sounds like the things that you and I talked about earlier, similar to Marx, in a way."

Wo had a quick mind. "But the difference is how we go about attaining this 'new creation'! You and I have talked about doing it through reeducation and laws. And we found that it does not work. But Li Ming showed me that I needed to ask Jesus Christ to forgive me of my offenses against him. He also explained that I needed to commit myself to following Jesus and being his disciple. He said that Jesus would change me into a new person on the inside."

"So what decision did you make, Wo?"

"I did just like he said. I have decided to believe in Jesus."

"Congratulations!" I said. I was beside myself with joy.

"Then you are now truly a 'New Man.' I am so happy for you, Wo!"

I was sitting on a chair next to him and he was leaning toward me. "Thank you, Dr. Kong," he said. "I want to learn more about this kind of life. Will you help me?"

"Of course. I'll do what I can."

"Wonderful! Then you will come to my house and visit with me?"

"Come to your house?" I asked. "What do you mean?"

"Oh, you have not heard?" he said with surprise. "I am being discharged tomorrow!" His eyes were bright and dancing. "I have been here for four months. That is long enough."

"I am glad to hear it!" I said. "When would you like for me to come?"

"Please come next Tuesday evening. I want you to meet my sons, also. They have heard a great deal about you."

"I'd enjoy that very much," I said. The sun was beaming through the window behind Wo Wei, and he looked splendid.

"But for right now, let's talk about this statement." He opened the Bible again and turned to a page and read, "But you will receive power when the Holy Spirit comes on you; and you will be my witnesses. . . ."

The following night I was on duty again. The emergency room was busy, and I had just finished admitting a man to the ward who had a burn on his leg. The clerk at the door came rushing toward me. "Quick! Come out here!" he called. I followed him, accompanied by one of the medical students.

Before us was a ghastly sight. A small ambulance was backing up with its rear doors open wide. Inside were two children covered with blood, and screaming. The driver hastily explained that the children had been riding on the platform of a three-wheel bike. A taxi had struck the bike head-on while they were both driving down the dark street. When I asked who had been pedaling, he only pointed at the children and said that they had lost their father.

The student had brought a cart out to us. We quickly placed the two of them onto it and rolled them inside. The first child was a boy who looked about two years old. He had a large gash on his scalp, but otherwise looked okay. I asked the nurse to hold pressure on the gash for a few minutes to stop the bleeding.

The second child did not look as well. There was a deep cut through her right arm. It was not bleeding badly, but she could not move her hand at all. When I tested her sensation, I found that she had no feeling in her arm below the place where it had been cut. My heart sank. Some of the nerves in her arm had been injured. I called the operating room and told them to get ready for her operation.

I returned to the first child and showed the medical student how to sew his scalp back together. We washed the wound with soap and cleaned it out with lots of water. Then the student injected the numbing medication into the boy's skin, but he screamed all the more. The student looked very frustrated.

"I have numbed his skin. He should not be feeling pain anymore!" he said. "What should I do?"

"You're right, of course, but he's scared," I replied. "Let's try to distract his attention." I picked up the bell of my stethoscope and twirled it in front of his face. He responded by crying more. Then the student joined in. He held up a pocket flashlight in front of the boy. At this, the boy stopped crying. He looked very interested. Reaching for the light, he fingered it carefully. Then he let out a giggle. The student started sewing up his scalp, the child totally engrossed with his new toy.

The student seemed to have things well in hand, so I left and walked toward the operating room. The trip took about five minutes and I passed through several deserted halls. I jumped when I heard my name spoken.

"Dr. Kong, I thought I might find you here!" called a sweet voice. I turned to find a woman standing in a corner of the hall. It was Fei Chow.

"I know that this is an unusual time to stop you. But you are such a busy man. I wanted to see you alone." She walked up to me, more sheepish than the first time she'd approached me with her strange proposal.

"Dr. Fei," I said, "this is not appropriate. You should not be meeting me at night like this. It is not good for our reputations." I was thinking about the little girl waiting for me in surgery.

"Reputation nothing!" she said bitterly. "I'm willing to sacrifice it all to get you! Have you thought about my offer?"

"Dr. Fei, there is nothing to think about," I said. "There is no way I can marry you. I know that you are in a difficult situation, but marrying me is not the answer. I will not do it."

Her attitude changed abruptly. "Difficult situation? You do not know the half of it! I am going to get out of China any way that I can. If I can't go with you, I will find another way!" She turned on her heel and walked off.

"Fei Chow," I called out, "don't do anything foolish!" She did not look back but kept walking away down the dark hall.

When I arrived in the operating room, the young girl was awake, lying on the operating table and clenching her teeth from the pain. I looked over her wound in the better light. We talked together as I cleaned it with soap.

"What is your name?" I asked.

"Dao Tung," she said softly. "What are you doing?"

"I am going to try to fix this big cut on your arm."

"Is it going to hurt?" she asked, whimpering.

"Not anymore." I had already anesthetized her arm without her realizing it. I put some cloth drapes over her chest and arm and began to explore the injury. The cut had severed her biceps muscle in half, but thankfully, it had missed the large artery that ran down the inside of her arm. I blotted the blood that was oozing and then saw what I was looking for: The nerve was lying before me—the one that gave sensation and movement to her lower arm.

The nerve was snow white and about as big around as a pencil. It was torn on one side only. I breathed a sigh of relief. If it had been completely cut, it would have been much more difficult to repair. The circulating nurse positioned a large magnifying glass over her arm so that I could see better. I realized that it would be difficult to repair the part that was torn. Even if I was successful, she might not recover any movement of her arm, but I had to try. Otherwise, she would certainly be crippled.

I took the tiny silk suture thread in one hand and threaded the needle. With my left hand I slowly picked up the nerve with forceps, and with the right hand I put the needle through the nerve. She gave a jump when I did so. I apologized for the pain she had felt. Then, in the same way, I put the needle through the other side of the nerve. I pulled the two ends of the nerve together and tied the first knot. Over the next hour I repeated this procedure several times. Finally, the nerve was put back together, but whether the tiny nerve fibers would heal remained to be seen. I repaired the cut muscles that lay over the nerve. Then, as morning dawned, I put in the skin stitches. While I was wrapping a dressing on her arm, Dao Tung asked me how long it would be before she could use it again.

"It will take several weeks to get better, but meanwhile, I want you to just play with your brother and don't worry about your arm." Even as I spoke, however, I worried for her. I didn't know whether she would recover any use of her arm at all.

When Tuesday night came, I got on my bike and started out to find Wo Wei's home. It was near the American Embassy, an area I knew quite well. The Embassy had shown American movies each month for the twenty-or-so U.S. citizens in Shanghai. There were some rather nice homes in the area compared to most of Shanghai.

When I arrived, I locked my bike to a tree and walked up a well-lit stairway. I felt a little anxious about how our evening would go, for I had never met Wo on his own territory before. I rang the doorbell and took in a deep breath.

The door opened. There stood Wo Wei, dressed like a typical Chinese. It seemed strange to see him out of his hospital gown. "Dr. Kong, welcome!" he said, leading me inside.

Wo's sons were seated on the sofa and stood when I entered. Wo introduced me to Jiang and Lang, then we sat at the table and Wo went to the kitchen to bring us some tea.

Jiang was the first to speak. "We want you to tell us about what has happened to our father," he said. "He is different now."

"What do you mean by 'different'?" I asked with a smile.

"Oh, I guess *happy* is the best word," said Jiang.

"He has decided to believe in Jesus Christ, and to follow his ways," I replied. Wo Wei returned with the cups of tea and gave one to each of us. Then he reached for the black Bible on his desk and set it out in front of us.

"Let's begin," he said. "Dr. Kong, I have been reading here about one of the things that Jesus said. I want to ask you about it. Jesus said, 'What good will it be for a man if he gains the whole world, yet forfeits his soul?' What does this mean?"

"I hope that you don't mind if we listen," said Jiang. "We are curious about these things as well."

"I am happy that you are here," I replied. I turned to Wo. "Jesus is saying that even if a person has a new bicycle and a color TV and many friends, what good will that do him after he dies?"

"I had not ever thought of that," said Lang. "We do not often think about an afterlife."

"There is something much more important than possessions," I said.

"I know what that is!" chimed in Wo Wei. "It is to receive God's forgiveness and allow him to transform your life!"

Lang leaned over and spoke quietly to Jiang, "Can you believe that our father is saying things like this?"

"That is absolutely right, Wo," I said. "What else have you learned?"

"I have been reading from the book of Acts about how the Christians lived. They ate their meals together and shared their possessions. They collected money to help anyone who had a problem."

"Dad, it sounds kind of like the Marxist ideals that you taught us about. What is the difference?" asked Lang.

Wo Wei looked pleased at the question. "The difference is inside. Jesus Christ can give us the power to really love one another, but we first have to have faith in him."

Then Jiang spoke, "The Marxists deny that God exists, so

how can they have the power it takes to have the ideal sort of society that they want?"

"Yes, that makes sense," said Lang, "but my friends will think that I am crazy if I become a Christian. It is just a fairy tale about a man."

"Can a fairy tale change the life of a man like your father?" I asked, looking at Wo. Lang had no reply.

Wo had some other questions for me. We talked about how Peter had accepted people of other races. Wo Wei confessed that he needed to change his attitude toward the Africans in Shanghai. He knew that he had not shown them much respect. He asked about why there were different groups of Christians fighting against one another in northern Ireland.

When the evening ended, his sons were sorry that we had to stop. We decided to meet again the following week.

"We have heard many strange things tonight," said Jiang. "We are grateful for the change we have seen in our father. He is like a different person."

Wo just smiled.

Dao Tung was not doing any better. Each morning before going to the operating room I'd examine her arm. The skin was healing well, but her hand was still limp. She could not move it at all. Furthermore, she had not recovered any sensation in her hand. I feared that the nerve was not healing. Rather, it might be turning into a large scar on the inside, as often happened in such cases.

She had discovered that her father had been killed in the wreck, but at age five, she did not really understand. It was just as well. For the time being, there were enough problems. I was grateful that her mother had stayed with Dao Tung constantly since the night of the wreck.

One day after surgery was completed, I went by to see Dr. Tao. He was usually in his office at midday and I found him there.

He greeted me with a bright smile. "Dr. Kong, I have good news for you!"

"What is that?" I replied.

"Today I repeated the bone marrow examination on the artist that you and I cared for last year. It shows no leukemia. He is in remission!"

"That's wonderful!" I remembered the way Zhange had cried in his room. "What will happen now?"

"I am going to let him go home for a while. He will be glad to hear that. So far, all that I've had for him has been bad news. I'd much rather tell him something that he can feel good about!"

"It does get depressing just talking about bad things," I agreed.

"But speaking of bad news, something very unusual happened today," said Tao, in a different tone. "It concerns one of our physicians, Fei Chow. I think that you worked with her before. She came in here and said that she was tired of living under suppression. She said that she had married a man who was visiting from Hong Kong."

"Oh, no!" I said.

"Yes, she did it. She is going to be leaving China next week, as soon as her visa comes through. What a desperate woman!"

"I wonder if she will find happiness?"

"I think not. There is suppression everywhere. It's not just in China. It's in America and Hong Kong also, because the suppression is the inward selfishness of humanity itself, not simply a political system."

"That is a pretty strong statement."

"But it is true," said Dr. Tao in a thoughtful voice. "I have been thinking about this."

I looked out the window. "I believe that I have found the solution to this problem, Dr. Tao."

"Oh, really?" He sounded interested. "You have indeed found an answer? How can I find out about it?"

"I'd like you to come with me to discuss this with another man, a former patient of ours."

"Who is that?"

"It is Wo Wei. You remember him."

"I certainly do. He is one of the Party leaders! Are you sure that it is safe to talk to him?"

Given his past, I could understand why Dr. Tao would be anxious about this invitation. "Wo is different now," I said. "He is a changed man. I think that you'd like to hear what he has to say. You will come?"

"Will you be there?"

"Of course."

"Then I will come. I have little to lose. Kong, you have certainly challenged my mind since you have come to China."

The following Tuesday, Dr. Tao rode beside me toward the Embassy street. I had called Wo Wei earlier to let him know that the two of us were coming. Wo seemed to be open to the idea. I could tell that Dr. Tao was anxious, and I was concerned about the outcome of the evening.

Wo Wei and his sons greeted us at the door. Dr. Tao and I sat down on the sofa. Jiang began the conversation in a lively mood.

"Dr. Kong, this has been a very interesting week. Father and I have read from the Bible every night after work, and I think that I am beginning to understand what it means."

Wo was beaming. "Jiang, would you explain it to Dr. Tao?

I think that he is interested in knowing about these things also."

"I will try," he replied. "The basic problem in the world is sin, or rebellion against God. This is why there are so many problems in society, even problems that we have seen in China."

Dr. Tao was listening intently. He looked at me as if to say, "Is it safe here?" I smiled at him reassuringly.

Jiang continued. "All of our own efforts to change human nature are confounded by this basic problem. That is why God sent a Savior to us, Jesus Christ. He is the one who can rescue us from this problem."

Dr. Tao broke in and looked at me, "You mean the same Jesus that the English who built the Third Hospital talked about?"

"Yes, the same one," I replied.

Jiang kept speaking. "What we need to do is to receive his forgiveness for this rebellion, and to decide to be his disciples."

"Do you know someone who has done this?" Dr. Tao inquired.

"Yes," replied Jiang, "My father!"

Dr. Tao was quite surprised. "You mean your father has become a Christian?"

Wo Wei turned toward him, his eyes glowing. "Yes, Dr. Tao. It is wonderful! My life has changed. My interests have changed. I have a new life now."

"But what about your revisions on the school books?" asked Lang skeptically. "When will you get around to finishing the revisions that you began?"

"Lang, my son, now I will really have something to write about!" Then he looked at Jiang, "You understand the Bible well. But have you made the decision to follow Jesus Christ yourself?"

It became very quiet in the room. We all looked at Jiang and he straightened up.

"Yes, Father. In my room last night I decided that I want this kind of life, too. I have found hope through believing in Jesus."

Wo jumped to his feet. "That is wonderful!" he exclaimed, "just wonderful!"

Dr. Tao was looking on in disbelief. He shook his head. "This is remarkable," he said to Wo. "I would never have thought that a man like you could believe such things."

Wo then posed a question, "And what about you, Dr. Tao? Is there room in your life for Jesus Christ?"

"All of this is very new to me," said Tao. "I will need some time to consider it. Actually, I did hear some things about Jesus when I was a student in the University, but that was forty years ago."

Then Wo Wei brought up an idea. "Dr. Kong, you know that I love China with all my heart. I want my country to grow strong. Do you suppose that there is a way that I could see how Christians actually live together as it says in the book of Acts?"

I did not know what to say. I thought for a moment, then an idea struck me. "Wo, I remember Li Ming telling me about his hometown. Why don't we go visit it? We may find what we are looking for!"

The following Sunday Wo and I met in front of the train station. We found the one going to Gao Lian and walked out onto the platform. I looked at the nicer cars up front for officials, but Wo did not seem to notice them. He climbed into a passenger car in back, and I followed.

It was very crowded inside, but we found a hard wood seat with some space, and sat down. There was a girl next to me who was reading from a school book. I looked over her shoulder and was amused to find that it was the same book that I had been using to study my language lessons. I began to read aloud along with her. As the train began to move, she noticed me and blushed. "Daddy," she asked the man next to her, "where is that man from?"

"I do not know, but I will ask." He looked up at me, "Sir, what country are you from?"

"Mei gou," I replied. I said to myself, *"Mei" means beautiful; "gou" means country. Yes, America is a beautiful country!*

It only took about thirty minutes to reach Gao Lian. Wo and I got off by ourselves at the small station and looked around. There was a little river that ran through the center of the town. I saw blue hills in the distance. It was just as Li Ming had described it. We were not sure where to go. There was no one standing around to ask, so Wo Wei and I just started to walk down the main street.

"Dr. Kong," said Wo Wei, "I have a concern. Are you aware that it is not permissible for members of the Communist Party to believe in God?"

"No, I didn't know that. But I'm not surprised. They do see things differently than Christians do."

"Yes. It is a matter of sworn allegiance. Strictly speaking, I should resign the Party because of my decision." He sounded as though he was in a fix. "But I feel that I have good news to share with the Party and with the country. My position as editor is influential."

"I see your dilemma, Wo." I thought about it while we

walked. "I do not know what would be best for you, but I will support your decision either way. It is difficult!"

Just then, we heard the sound of singing. Wo turned to me and said, "Christians sing, don't they?"

"Yes, they do," I replied. "They probably sing everywhere in the world."

We followed the sound and found it to be coming from a hollow in a hillside where about one hundred people had gathered. They were sitting on the grass. Wo and I found a dry spot in back of them as they sang several more songs. Then a man stood up. All of the people listened intently to what he was saying.

"My name is Yao Guang. Some of you who are older know me, but many of you will find me to be a new face here. I was recently released from prison; in fact, it was just two months ago. I was there for eighteen years."

Wo Wei leaned close to me and asked, "What could a Christian man do that would warrant a sentence in prison?"

The man continued, "During the Cultural Revolution, I was the pastor of this church. We were meeting each week in this very place, as we had for years. The people of our community were constantly refreshed by the love of Jesus Christ that was shared among us. But I and several others were arrested without warning one day. We were accused of being subversive to the government, for we had been teaching things that our leaders did not agree with, though we meant no harm. They locked us away without a trial. There were only twenty of us in this church then. I was worried about what might happen to all of you. I was concerned about how your faith would endure those hard years." The people were looking on intently. "But today I see so many more in our church than ever before! May God be honored for sustaining us all through these years of trial!"

Wo looked around. "You mean all of these people are Christians? What a wonderful thing!"

The man continued to relate how Jesus Christ had given him strength to survive in the prison. He told of how he had been informed that his wife was dead and how he had wept. He also talked about the day that he was released. Before he left he told his captors how they, too, could be released from sin through the love of Jesus.

After he finished speaking, the people started to stand and a man near us came over and introduced himself.

"Welcome to the Gao Lian church!" he said. He asked our names and we told him how we had come to visit them. He asked us to join him for lunch with some others in his home.

As we walked toward his house, Wo whispered to me, "This is very unusual! He does not even know us, and yet he is inviting us to have a meal with him. This is very unlike the Chinese. Do Christian people do this often?"

I replied, "Remember how the people in the book of Acts acted toward each other?"

"Yes. They shared their possessions with one another. They ate together, and they were very happy. You know, Kong, this church is like a model for the society that Jesus talked about!"

When we arrived at the man's home, I was surprised to see about a dozen others gathered together. We all sat down and our host said that he was going to pray and ask Jesus to show kindness to the visitors. The food was passed around and we began to eat. The people were laughing and enjoying one another's company.

I could not help but notice that one of the women at the large table looked very familiar. She must have seen me looking at her, for she spoke to me.

"Yes, Dr. Kong. I know you also. I am the widow of Li Ming."

"I had wondered if I might see you here," I said. I immediately introduced her to Wo Wei.

"I owe so much to your husband!" he said. "He gave me the message that changed my life. He was a wonderful man."

"Thank you, Wo," she replied. "He often told me about his conversations with you after he would return from the hospital. But you should know that Li was not always so kind. When we were younger, he drank very much and cursed. He had no thought of anything but making money."

"I find that hard to believe. He was really like that? What changed him?"

She explained: "We lived in Shanghai during the Cultural Revolution, but food was scarce and our house had been robbed. So we moved out to Gao Lian. We had nothing but the clothes we wore when we arrived. We were very hungry, but the people of the church showed us great kindness. One man let us live in his home with him. Another gave us some of his clothes. He and his wife were both Christians. So were most of the others in our town. Over the weeks we listened to them all talk about Jesus Christ. We saw the love that they had for us and each other. It was not long before we, too, became followers of Jesus."

Wo interrupted, "And how long did it take for Li to change his behavior? A few months?"

"He began to change almost at once. But Jesus had been working in his life for years to develop the man whom we knew. It took a long time. I miss him with all of my heart," she said, "but, Wo, we will meet him again!"

On the train going back to Shanghai that evening, Wo and I sat quietly for a while. "Dr. Kong, I'd like to go back to visit them again," Wo said at last. "I learned today that being a Christian will not always be easy."

"Yes, it can be difficult. There are some who will oppose you," I said.

"I will remain strong, Dr. Kong," he said. "I know that soon you will go back to America, and I may never see you again, but I will not forget the decision I have made or the things I saw today."

And I thought, *Neither will I!*

I had begun packing my belongings, trying to pare them down to fill only two suitcases. I had collected so many gifts that I had no place for them all. I regretted that I'd have to leave some behind.

One day I received a telegram from home. It read, "Missing you—your family." My heart jumped! I had been gone too long.

When I returned to the ward one morning, I made an encouraging discovery. Dao Tung lifted her arm less awkwardly than she had before. This time she even lifted her fingers—only slightly—but it was a sign that the nerve was healing! I was excited, but tried not to show it too much. I did not want to get the little girl's hopes up higher than I should. She was not in the clear yet.

I had lunch that day with Keith at the Jing Jiang Hotel. He was going to stay on for another year and continue to study the Chinese language. We sat, drinking green tea, and talked about what we had learned in China.

"You and I are privileged to be allowed to live here for so long. They are a friendly people," I said. "I would not mind coming back someday."

"Will you, Nicholas?" Keith asked, looking over at me.

"I'd love to! But in the meantime, I can be their ambassador in America, so to speak. That was one of the reasons I came."

Keith observed, "It takes the Chinese a long time to trust one another, but once they do, they're committed friends for life."

"They have some things to teach us," I said. "In America, people move around so much that they usually do not have time to develop deep relationships. But more than this, I am impressed at the impact of ideas here."

"What do you mean?" asked Keith, as he looked over our bill.

"Ideas are strong, really strong—stronger than armies. They shape almost everything that we do."

"That seems obvious to me," Keith agreed. "So what is your point?"

"In both America and China there are injustices. In our country we have tried to answer the problem through giving political freedoms, but we are still bound by our individual selfishness. In China, much of the opposite is the case. They have restricted freedoms in hope of liberating people from their own selfishness. We have had an opportunity to actually see the impact of Marxist ideas. It has been one of the most impressive information campaigns in history. People like you and me can look and decide for ourselves whether they have succeeded."

"Do you think that they did?"

We got up to leave and I said, "To a small extent they have, but what they have really done is to create a great void, an empty place in the hearts of many people. The question for the next generation is 'Who will fill this void?'"

"Nicholas, I believe you are right." Keith reached out to shake my hand. "It has been good knowing you. Maybe we will meet here again and see the outcome. I would not be surprised. We both will probably still have some adventure in us even after our time here."

Dr. Tao, Wo Wei, his sons, and I continued to meet at his home for the last few weeks before I was to leave. They and Dr. Tao, in particular, asked a lot of questions. And Wo usually had good answers for the questions. I was sorry when our last evening together came, for I knew that I would miss these men.

That evening the four of us were looking over the new Bibles that Wo had bought.

"Where did you get these, Father?" asked Jiang. He was surprised to see the Bibles. "They look so new and attractive."

"I bought them at the bookstore," replied Wo. "I am happy to find that the government has made them available to us now. Most of them had already been sold. There were several other people trying to buy them also. It was exciting to see!"

Tao looked through one and then turned to Wo. "Can I have this one?" he asked.

"Why certainly! I got one for each of us," said Wo. He was not anticipating the next statement from Dr. Tao.

"There is a reason why I want one of these. I have thought a lot about this faith. I have made a decision. I want to believe in Jesus Christ also. I want to experience this life that I see in you!"

Wo was beside himself with joy. "This is wonderful!" he said, jumping to his feet. "Now you and I are brothers, even with my son. There are three of us!"

After we finished our discussion for the evening, I asked Wo Wei the whereabouts of his other son, Lang.

"He does not want to join us anymore. He told me that he can not believe the things we do."

"This must make you sad, Wo," I said.

Wo Wei looked a little troubled, but then brightened up. "I am sorry for him, but I am encouraged at the prospects for the future!"

"What prospects?" I asked.

"Dr. Kong, I have decided to stay in the Party, at least as long as they will accept me. I want to share with them the good news that I have learned. It will be good for all of China!"

The next morning I returned to the hospital for my last day of work. Surgery had been canceled for the day. They were going to have a going-away party for me instead. I went to the ward to see what I had left undone. Dao Tung called me over as soon as I arrived.

"Dr. Kong," she said in her high voice, "look at this!"

She stretched out the arm that I had repaired weeks ago. I was not expecting much to happen. Then, to my surprise, she opened and closed her hand! She did it again and again.

"Terrific!" I said in English.

"What does that mean?" she asked.

"It means that I am very happy for you," I said. I gave her a big, warm hug. Dr. Shi called me from the door.

"Where are you going? Are you going to leave us?" Dao asked me.

"Yes, I am going back to my country."

"Is it far away? Will I get to see you again?"

"It is very far away, Dao. Someday I will come back, and you will be a grown woman then."

Dr. Shi whistled for me. I waved good-bye to Dao, fighting back a tear as I walked out. We headed for the meeting hall.

Almost all the hospital's doctors turned out for the event: Dr. Cheng, Dr. Tao, and three dozen others. I was impressed to see that several of the nurses and technicians were there also. We sat around a big table and ate ice cream and drank orange juice, special treats for us all. With much feeling, each of the doctors I had worked with stood in turn, from the eldest to the youngest, and told of their impressions of me. Dr. Cheng then presented me with a diploma. It was covered with several official seals and had a number in the upper right hand corner. To my amusement, it read "001."

But the most touching farewell came from the elderly woman who had watched my bike in front of the hospital. When I handed her my ticket on the way out, she pressed a small package into my hand. "I want to thank you for coming to live in China! You are now truly our friend." As I pedaled, I wondered how she could possibly have afforded to give me a gift. I opened the package. Her gift was a plastic ink pen— one half of a day's wages. She had given what she could.

Back at the dorm I had a few minutes before the van came to take me to the airport. I climbed the staircase and ladder onto the roof and looked over Shanghai for the last time.

"I can't believe that I actually did this," I said aloud. "Who would believe it?" I pulled out the notebook that I had carried up with me. In it was an unfinished letter to Pao Chu in Hong Kong. I was going to mail it to him, for I would not be seeing him on the way home. I sat down on a sun-bleached chair and wrote:

> When I was in Hong Kong with you, we talked about why people are often so unfair to one another, and how this has not changed, even in our modern times. What is the solution? I came to China wondering and hoping to find it. Pao Chu, I realize what the answer is now. It is not a social or political change that is needed so much as an inner, spiritual change. Let me tell you what I have found. . . .